HITCHHIKING TO INDIA IN 1962

INDIA, THE BALKANS AND GREECE IN 2015

JOHN WALLER

Based on the diaries of
ANDREW MACALPINE

YIANNIS BOOKS

HITCHHIKING TO INDIA IN 1962

Copyright © 2015 John Waller

All rights reserved. No part of this book may be reproduced, transmitted or stored in any form or by any means without the prior permission of the publisher except for quotations of brief passages in reviews.

Published in 2016 by **YIANNIS BOOKS**
101 Strawberry Vale, Twickenham, TW1 4SJ UK
Tel. 0044 2088923433, 0044 7811351170

Typeset by Mike Cooper, 25 Orchard Rd, Sutton SM1 2QA
Printed by Antony Rowe, Chippenham, Wiltshire

www.yiannisbooks.com
'True stories of history, drama and romance'

208 pp
ISBN 978-0-9547887-8-0

To Andrew

A great hitchhiking buddy
and lifelong friend

Mahatma Gandhi was born in Porbandar, Gujarat on October 2nd 1869. On January 30th 1948 he was assassinated in New Delhi by a Hindu nationalist, who opposed Gandhi's fasts for peace, his conciliatory policy towards Muslims and his peace overtures to Pakistan.

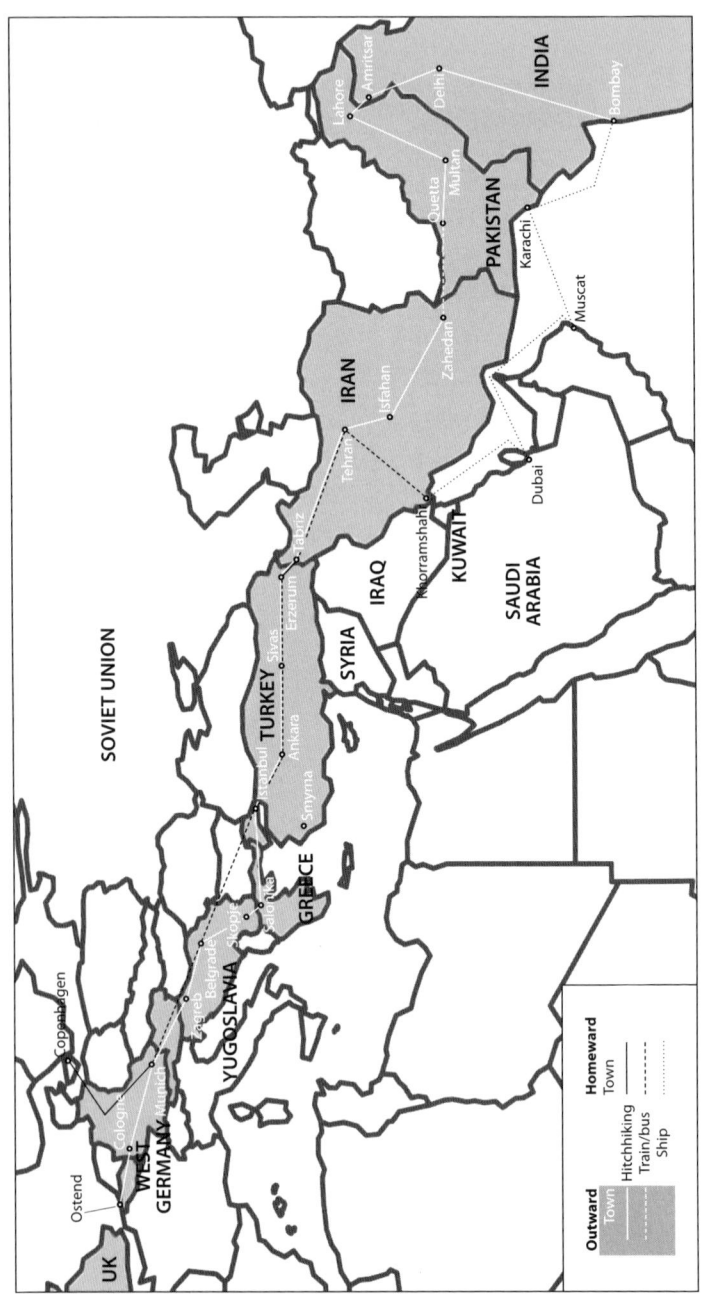

CONTENTS

	Acknowledgements	8
	Introduction	10
1.	'Don't mention the war' Basil Fawlty	14
2.	Western Europe before Schengen	17
3.	Yugoslavia and secret police	22
4.	Greece, occupation and civil war	29
5.	Istanbul, Turks and Greeks	39
6.	Turkey and Armenians	53
7.	Iran to Tehran after the CIA Coup	68
8.	South Iran or Afghanistan?	79
9.	Andrew compares Turkey and Iran	100
10.	Pakistan and Partition	106
11.	Amritsar and the Sikhs	121
12.	Delhi, tea with Indira Gandhi	126
13.	Agra, Ajanta, Ellora and on	133
14.	Bombay at last	146
15.	Homeward bound up the Persian Gulf	152
16.	India fifty years on	159
17.	The Balkans in 2015, refugees and Syria	174
18.	Three days that saved the Euro	187
19.	Life in a financial Greek tragedy	195
	An open letter to Chancellor Merkel	203
	Books by John Waller	206

ACKNOWLEDGMENTS

Andrew's diaries have been waiting to be published for 53 years and without them there would be no book. 1962 was before the hippies started travelling to India and, whilst they might have had experiences, which we knew little about, Andrew's observations remain invaluable. Today a similar journey would be almost impossible to repeat, not only because strife has ruled out much of the route but also hitchhiking is a forgotten means of travel.

My thoughts at the end of each chapter are based on many years reading. I chose from my extensive library what I considered were the most valuable books on the countries we visited. I thank the authors, who fired my enthusiasm to finish this book. These are:

Yugoslavia – *The Balkans, 1804–1999, Nationalism, War and the Great Powers* by Misha Glenny.

Greece – *Inside Hitler's Greece, the Experience of Occupation, 1941–44* by Mark Mazower.

The Greeks and the Turks – *Paradise Lost, Smyrna 1922, the Destruction of Islam's City of Tolerance* by Giles Milton.

Turks and Armenians – *The Armenian Massacres in Ottoman Turkey, A Disputed Genocide* by Guenter Lewy and *Rebel Land – Among Turkey's Forgotten Peoples* by Christopher de Bellaigue.

Iran – *All the Shah's Men, An American Coup and the Roots of Middle East Terror* by Stephen Kinzer and *Mussadiq's Memoirs: the End of the British Empire in Iran*.

Pakistan and Partition – *The Great Partition, the Making of India and Pakistan* by Yasmin Khan.

India and Sikhs – *Amritsar, Mrs Gandhi's Last Battle* by Mark Tully and Satish Jacob.

Authors need friends to comment on their books as they progress through each draft. I would therefore like to thank:

My brother Richard: 'The book won't sell; I liked the diaries but you write for the thinking man.' 'And woman!' added my sister-in-law Valerie in the background.

They are right, I am a thinker and my thoughts appear at the end of each chapter.

Betty, my company and my political secretary: 'I'm ploughing through it.'

Charles Henderson CB, my companion on the Corfu Trail, ex-senior civil servant and actuary: 'I am not going to criticise your arithmetic.'

Olwen Thomas: 'An interesting read.'

Lucy O'Sullivan: 'A fascinating, delightful and enjoyable read.'

Louise Etherington, our daughter: 'Wow, you were young once, hard to believe sometimes. Andrew rocks!'

Julie Archer: 'The further you travel, the more enjoyable it becomes'.

INTRODUCTION

My original subtitle for the book was 'Through Empires, old and new'. It then became: 'The Tragedy of Empires'. The word 'Empire' was to be loosely read. It would end with a comment on the future of the European Union.

Andrew and I travelled first through Western Europe before it became the European Community. We entered Yugoslavia through the old Austro-Hungarian Empire, and moved south through what could be called the Serbian Empire into the old Ottoman Empire. Twenty years before our journey in 1942 the Croats set out to either exterminate all the Orthodox Serbs and Jews or forcibly convert the former to Catholicism. Later the Serbs would massacre the Muslims in Srebrenica.

Through family tales and travels, I knew a little about Greece and remembered that forty years before our journey in 1922, which was then in living memory, there had been a tragic desire to create 'The New Byzantine Empire'. 1.3 million Christians were expelled from the new Turkey in exchange for 480,000 Muslims that had to leave Greece. It didn't matter whether they could speak the language of their new country; all that mattered was their religion. Today those Muslims that lived in Thrace and were exempt from the deportations live alongside their Christian neighbours without rancour.

Turkey was of course the heart of the Ottoman Empire, but we were to pass by the Old Russian Empire, whose expansion led to the demise of Anatolian Armenia. In 1915 in Eastern Turkey, over 600,000 Orthodox Armenians lost their lives when they were deported to the Syrian desert beside the River Euphrates, where ISIS are now based. This represented over a third of the pre-war Anatolian Armenian population. Sunni Turks, Kurds and Circassians were involved in the massacres of the refugees. The Shia Alevi would also suffer from the dominant Sunnis but in many cases they saved the Christian Armenians.

Iran could claim a long history of the Persian Empire, but I became more interested in the US fear of the Soviet Empire, which led to the start of the American Empire.

We would end our great adventure in India just 14 years after the end of the two-hundred-year-old British Empire. 9/11 still seems just like yesterday to us. It is in fact 14 years ago. And it was just 14 years before we arrived in India where, during partition, 12 million people became refugees because of their religion: they were Hindu, Muslim and Sikh. Between ½ and 1 million died in the brutal circumstances of ethnic cleansing.

In England, we learn about Tudor, Elizabethan and Georgian history. For many these represent just styles of architecture. We are rich in the fabric of our buildings. In the countries we passed through, their history is ingrained in their hearts, handed down from generation to generation. Tragically it is the stories of hate rather than love that are passed on.

I hope, for all the horror my story tells, there is a little love in it as well: Andrew's affectionate relationship with all those he met and my postcards to Jannie, my Danish girl friend whom I later married.

In 2014, Jannie and I made a remarkable trip from Southampton to Japan and back. Between Britain and Japan, we encountered a multitude of religions. Belief is good, but using religion to generate hate is an abomination.

In Morocco, on the outskirts of Tetouan we came to the huge Muslim cemetery. Nearby there was a Catholic cemetery and a Jewish cemetery. These three communities had lived in harmony for centuries. We found this elsewhere in Islamic countries within the old Ottoman Empire where the vast emigration of Sephardic Jews settled after their persecution by the Catholic conquistadors in the Iberian Peninsula. We experienced the same in Tunisia, including a wonderful visit to the Bardo museum to see the mosaics and Carthage, where armed police on the beach protected us tourists from possible attack by terrorists. In both Morocco and Tunisia there are still significant Jewish minority communities. Tragically, since Western military involvement in the Middle East, all this harmony is breaking down.

Unlike what we read in some of the press, I believe that individual Muslims are tolerant and decent people and want to live in peace with their neighbours.

All of us have family history, which influences our views. This is mine. In the First World War my Irish father had fought up through Palestine with General Allenby to defeat the Ottomans. Returning to Ireland, he talked about the war with his wife, who said: 'I'm an English woman and, according to your brother Harry's rant last week, if my country isn't bombing the Kurds with mustard gas, it's burning down reed-hutted villages wiping out people wherever it goes. The truth is we want to safeguard oil in Persia to keep a hold on India! What do the Kurds even want?'

My father replied: 'Independence.'

She continued: 'Could it happen here in Ireland? I feel the change from people as they look at me. They know that Britain won't give Ireland its freedom. Then the Arabs and the Kurds and the Indians would all have to be given theirs too.'

My father, nominally Church of Ireland, had nationalist sympathies. In those days, Protestants and Catholics fought on the Republican side. Religion created, and then poisoned, the new divided country, just as it would in India at Independence.

INTRODUCTION

In June 1940, I became a refugee in my own country. At the age of just six weeks, my parents uprooted our home and in a minute caravan took their three sons to Cornwall, where my father moved into a chicken coop. We had been living in East Kent over which the Battle of Britain would soon be fought and the talk was of Hitler invading Britain. From early days I wanted peace in Europe.

In September 1962 at the end of our great hitchhike, I was reunited with Jannie and, less important in my life's journey but more significant for this book, heard, whilst travelling along a German autobahn, the extraordinary claim: *'Adenauer lieber De Gaulle'*. This sealed my love for Europe.

I end this book with a look at the places we visited 50 years on. The chapter on India today is happy and tells how I found so much that reminded me of 1962.

The next chapter looks at the Balkans. I have recently visited three Balkan countries recovering from a tragic civil war and now struggling with the mass migration of peoples from the countries along our hitchhiking trail.

I conclude with the horror of the situation in Greece, which Northern Europeans cannot comprehend. It could fatally damage the European Union of which I am an ardent supporter.

There is a lot of history in the book. I do not apologise for that. Churchill said: 'The further back you go, the further forward you can see'.

CHAPTER 1
'DON'T MENTION THE WAR'
BASIL FAWLTY

'Don't mention the War!' John Cleese, aka Basil Fawlty, will be forever remembered for his goosestep and this reference to his German guests at Fawlty Towers. I will remember John and his best friend Alan for a more important reason.

'I know the perfect girl for you,' claimed Alan as we were wandering through Cambridge in March 1962. 'She's a Dane.'

'Dane or Dutch, they are all the same to me: exotic. Tell me more.'

'Jannie is a red-head.'

'I'm in love with her already.'

We walked on to the hostel where Alan's girl friend was living and I was introduced to Jannie. She was the most beautiful girl I had ever met. I still think so over 50 years on. Jannie would go on to become the third character in our great adventure hitchhiking to India. Playing off-stage, she would become the link with home: in every city, I would rush into the centre and visit the post office. If a letter were there, I would be over the moon. If not, I would be morose and return to my companion, Andrew, with fears of her falling in love with some handsome Dane.

So when did this crazy idea of hitchhiking to India start? After a round of golf at Royal Worlington, the University team turned their minds away from freezing East Anglia to the long Vac and a chance to relax in the sun.

'I'm thinking of going overland to India,' I claimed.

'In Andrew's Austin Healey 3000?' some wit suggested.

This open-top roadster would have been the perfect vehicle except for one major problem. It was so low-slung that a pebble could damage its under parts. Andrew's father was comparatively well off. They lived in Maida Vale and Andrew had been educated at a public school, the Perse in Cambridge. My Irish father had died when I was 9 and my mother had raised three boys by selling *Encyclopaedia Britannica* to the families of East Kent coal miners. I was a 'grammar-grub'.

'You no longer have your scooter,' the wit added.

My Lambretta 150 had already been sold to pay for a fine: my lanky Irish friend Brian had 'borrowed' a policeman's hat during our first rag day. The little fellow had gone in chase and had collided with myself, an innocent bystander. And so my wheels, hard earned from working as a teacher before going up, had to be sold. From then on, I would cadge a lift to the golf matches with those with cars.

'I'm going to hitchhike.' I sipped my glass of milk and ate some wonderful chocolate cake.

The assembled golfers, drinking their pints, fell about in mirth. 'Why India?'

'Because I hitched round North America last year, from New York to Los Angeles via Mexico, then to San Francisco and back to Miami via New Orleans and finally via Canada to New York. Last year I went west, this year I want to go east. Will anyone come?'

Silence fell. Then Andrew volunteered. 'Why not? And I will write a diary of the trip.' Andrew was literate: he was reading English. I was illiterate and pretending to read Maths. But I was numerate.

Laughter erupted at the thought of Andrew swapping his Austin Healey for his thumb.

'India is a hell of a long way away,' claimed the wit quite accurately.

'My first lift out of New York was 2,400 miles to Tuscon,

Arizona,' I replied, 'though the sign I had held up at the tunnel under the Hudson had said: "California". That's nearly the distance from Dunkirk to Istanbul, or the length of Iran.'

'So what will your sign say this time? Delhi?'

'No, English.'

'Or Scottish,' added Andrew Macalpine.

'But the Iranians can't read that! You must write it in Persian, with all its squiggles.' The golfers were becoming less cynical.

'I'll be the linguist,' suggested Andrew, who had spent a year at the Sorbonne.

After graduation – I scraped a third – we took the bus to Folkestone to say good-bye to my mother and then the ferry from Dover to Ostend.

CHAPTER 2
WESTERN EUROPE BEFORE SCHENGEN

Sunday 1st July

Arrived Ostend about 2.00. Got hitch with Belgian to Brussels. (1st over!) 3 in back of 4-seater with luggage – very cramped. His philosophy – I make a journey, I have work. Why not give lift? He was, however, very heavy and teutonic.

Arrived Bruxelles. Student who had travelled with us very helpful – if dissipated. We ate late lunch in bus shelter in middle of Bruxelles – pestered a little by tramp.

Bussed out of Bruxelles and hitched to Louvain. From Louvain to Liège where we tried to get hitch out of town and were picked up by two people, who took us to camp site just outside town but 25 minutes up hill from the main road!!

Anyway we camped first night, not good – rain. Women in bar whose English we flattered made our remaining 9 Belgian francs into 2 beers – very kind.

Monday 2nd July

Up at 5.00! Had lift from many of the English at the camp.

Got very good lift to Cologne – English serviceman and his wife.

We now started to hitch on Autobahn – much more difficult. We were left in wrong place at Cologne and only through a crash and John's initiative did we get a lift to Frankfurt with two boyos out for fun with Frankfurt women.

HITCHHIKING TO INDIA IN 1962

We then got fabulous lift with some German, who hadn't intended to give us a lift at all. He stopped to look at his map and was immediately surrounded by two hobos! He took us north of Karlsruhe to beginning of a Stuttgart autobahn.

We arrived in industrial Stuttgart in middle of rush hour and the rain. Went to public lats where wonderful devout Catholic woman gave us a St. Peter's medallion, water, a lemon and bread and some special healing liquid. Thus fortified by goodness we got out of Stuttgart in the rain.

We were then picked up by a charming German and his girl, who took us onto Munich Autobahn entirely for their own pleasure.

We slept night under Autobahn bridge, 10 yards from railway line and 15 from road!! Very noisy and cold. Camp fire, omelette. (John's a great cook.)

Tuesday 3rd July

Up late – 6.00! Met French girl hiking alone to Israel! Lift with American to Munich. Stop at Transport café on way. Pornographic literature. From the wireless came 'Openness of Spirit'.

In Munich went to get John's rucksack mended. They did it for nothing! Fortunately there was a French lady in shop who could act as interpreter. She had body in Germany, heart in France. Trousers stitched by *fraulein*!!

Outside Munich, first Austrian lift – a DS19!! What comfort. Arrive Austrian customs. (Did 100 on Autobahn.)

Left Germany and Belgium with no money! Spent £1 in Germany.

Arrived Salzburg – it is pouring with rain. We eventually find a youth hostel where we have a very good cheap meal and night's sleep. We meet our competitor in the race for India. Our plans for India laughed at derisively by Englishman who took 2 days from Liezen to Salzburg!

Wednesday 4th July

Up at 6.00 and soon on road. Various lifts take us to Liezen.

In afternoon very long lift from salesman takes us 60km from Graz. We are dropped and get another lift almost immediately. In Graz we eat lunch by the river at about 4.00 and push on to Jugoslavia.

Are given mad lift to the border by crazy Austrian driver. We are dropped off at border and try hitching.

John's card from Stuttgart, Germany, 6.00 Monday

Andrew's beard is pink and mine is blue. Dig that, Jannie dear. Hitching (*autostop*) – *sehr gut*.
Deutch gut – everything *gut*.
Rained last night and nobody got wet! Peter's tent is very good.
Soon in Austria, will scribble again soon.
Love John

John's thoughts on Western Europe

My memories are of course blurred; it is over 50 years ago. Andrew's journal is hilarious, but I want to mention a few critical moments of our trip. The twentieth century has treated the countries we passed through with great cruelty. Often these critical moments refer to some tragedy in history. I hope you, the reader, will put up with my thoughts. I was greatly privileged to make this journey, which today might not have been possible.

'Don't mention the War,' John Cleese joked. Tragically though, much of my story has to mention wars: the Balkan Wars; the collapse of the Ottoman Empire in the First World War and afterwards the Greeks trying to recapture their

Byzantine Empire; later the German occupation of Greece in the Second World War and the civil war that followed; the Russian-Turkish war and the Armenian tragedy; the start of the American Empire in Iran in fear of the Soviets in the Cold War; and finally the collapse of the British Empire after the Second World War and the tragic partition of India and Pakistan. My 'Thoughts' will follow Andrew's diary entries and expand on the history, so those preferring comedy to tragedy may choose to miss out my writing.

In 1962, hitchhiking in Western Europe was easy. The new Europeans wanted to meet and make friends with other nationalities, with some of whom they had been at war just 17 years before. Andrew with his fluent French and smattering of German entertained our hosts on every lift.

Overland travel, on the other hand, had complications that we do not have today, though border controls could be back soon because of the refugee crisis. There were national borders to be crossed, controls to be overcome, visas to be checked and passports to be stamped. As we will see later, when we left Yugoslavia the red tape at the border offered opportunities for bribery.

Queues of trucks waited for customs clearance. This arrangement was, however, excellent for hitchhikers. We could chat up the drivers and hope to get a lift. The Schengen Agreement, which enabled free movement of people and products throughout Western Europe, was then no more than a dream.

We didn't have credit cards in 1962 but had to carry travellers' cheques, which we exchanged for the local currency. The simplicity of one European currency was still 37 years in the future. Trade within the EEC is now almost as simple as trade within one's own country; there's just an extra box to complete on one's VAT return.

Europe was divided between Capitalist West and Communist East. The Marshall Plan in 1948, which offered economic assistance to European states in return for acceptance of liberal democracy, capitalism and American market penetration, not only enabled countries to rebuild after the Second World War, it lubricated the freedom of trade (at least for the US), which drove Western Europe forward. To secure the capitalist countries, NATO had been introduced in 1949. Austria, our last country before our entry into Communist Yugoslavia, was just seven years old after the end of occupation by the allied powers, America, Britain, France and Russia, each of which had its own zone. It had a capitalist economy, supported by the Marshall Plan, but politically it was neutral and certainly not a member of either NATO or the Warsaw Pact, the Soviet's response to the US.

CHAPTER 3
YUGOSLAVIA AND SECRET POLICE

Wednesday 4th July

After a few amusing conversations in Jugoslav, we get in with man going to Maribor.

We start to walk towards Verazadin road and walk into a catholic church. We hear music and go to town square where our hats and general strange demeanour soon distract everyone's attention from the pleasant music of a brass band. In no time at all we are surrounded by about 80 Yugoslav children all wanting to teach us their language. With the aid of phrase book we had the most remarkable and stimulating half hour in their company. How delightful children are.

We then get a lift out from Maribor at 8.00 to look for somewhere to sleep. We are left on the road to Zagreb but in a position whereby we have to hitch further out of town to sleep. (About 9.00) meet a couple of drunks (festival in Maribor), who tried to take John's camera. Policeman tries to help us. Eventually we sleep in adjacent railway buildings. Very comfortable and eventful first night in Yugoslavia.

Thursday 5th July

Up at 4.30. Lift to Zagreb by lunch in Mercedes!

In Zagreb we meet 2 Yugoslavs who take us back to their miserable flat and entertain us wonderfully with Slivovitch. They are very kind. Introduce us to their friends. Give us Yugoslav tea. Reluctance to talk about politics. We leave them about 2.30.

After half an hour we get lift in enormous American car driven by Belgian meat buyer – rather an embittered man – obviously pretty rich – had spent year looking for a dog for his wife. He found one and his wife died 5 months later. During the whole 3½ hours it took to cover the 242 miles from Zagreb to Belgrade he never asked anything about ourselves and told us little about himself. He talked a great deal about Yugoslavia.

As we drove across the enormous plain that lies between Zagreb and Belgrade I don't think I have seen anything more desolate. The whole route at intervals was lined by the tiny dwellings of the people who farmed the barren soil. The land was completely flat, in many places nothing more than marshland and always there were the poverty stricken hand-waving peasants tending their one or two cows like children.

We arrived Belgrade and immediately noticed the change in atmosphere. They were much colder. We camped in a park on the edge of Belgrade and fortunately were not disturbed even though we cooked over a camp fire – not disturbed that is until morning when rain got us smartly out of bed at 4.00.

John's card from Zagreb, Yugoslavia, Thursday lunch

Dragi Jannie
Alija bin hila vilo zadavoljna provesti kod vas jedno vece id uce sedmice ako Vam bude zgodno.
In case you are no good at Serbo-Croatian, this means: I want to spend an evening with you next week. We are now in Zagreb. The Yugoslavs are the most wonderful people we've seen. Very poor, but cheerful, friendly and helpful. We should be in Ankara on Monday or Tuesday. Hope you get home safely. Will write again very soon.
Grli vas John. Andrew sends regards.

HITCHHIKING TO INDIA IN 1962

Friday 6th July

Started hitching immediately and made pretty good headway. The further south we got the poorer the people. A stay for two hours in the middle of the day opposite a dead and ignored dog gave us some taste of things to come.

At the beginning of the next village saw woman suckling her baby at the side of the road. We got stuck in this godforsaken village after 20 km ride in lorry – all night effort.

We eventually got just outside Skopje on the road for following morning. Our early arrival was greeted by all the local children – just as sweet and vindictive as ours. They were certainly fascinated by us and there was one very sweet girl who kept wanting to play ball with me. There was also a little kid who brought us food for the fire. However, they were rather irritating and we were relieved when an older boy came and chased the others away. The sinister star on his shirt made one feel vaguely uncomfortable.

More uncomfortable-making was the all night work party working to the accompaniment of their own singing on the hill above our campsite. They were building the new *autoput*. However to make up for this we had our first night under the stars. Above the Milky Way and all around mountainous peaks. The perfect night sky and the coldness of mid-morning (3 a.m.) seemed to us the first signs of the Orient.

Saturday 7th July

Up at 5.00 and got our first lift as we had the previous day in a jeep taking people to work.

Then came a lorry and after a lift with a most pathetic chinless Yugoslav who had been Serbian tennis champion in 1929. He was apparently too poor to go away on holiday this year and yet had a fairly good job as lawyer in a medium sized town. He was perhaps the obvious example of oppression at work for he appeared caught in a web – almost desperate.

After lift with Persian students we came to frontier and came across the system at work. Because we could not produce some piece of paper which had never existed, the Yugoslav customs wanted to impound our money and make us sign a form by which we could claim the money from a bank in Belgrade if we produced the piece of paper which had never existed! At the end of a heated argument we kept our money but rather lost our good opinion of Yugoslavia.

John's thoughts on Yugoslavia

Yugoslavia offered a new dimension. What seemed to us a utopia, a Federation of six Republics – Slovenia, Croatia, Serbia, Bosnia, Montenegro and Macedonia, happily married under non-Soviet Communism and led by Tito – hid deep historical animosity. We entered through Slovenia, part of which in the 1920 plebiscite had voted to remain in Austria.

Andrew was in his element in Yugoslavia. Everything was '*dobar* this' and '*dobro* that'. Yugoslavia seemed to have a unified language, Serbo-Croat, or Serbo-crunch as we called it. We did not know that this would also lead to trouble as Croat intellectuals, including the future Croat nationalist and strongman, Franjo Tudjman, argued that the language was really a variant of Serbian and that Croatian was becoming a regional dialect. My contribution to this linguistic adventure was to call each of our hosts, 'Fangio', which brought out the machismo in the driver and terrified the living daylights out of Andrew.

Our first indication of disharmony was in Zagreb, capital of the Croatian republic, where there was a reluctance to talk about politics. This reluctance to talk could have been for fear of the civilian security service, which was mainly a Serbian institution, under the leadership of Aleksandar Rankovic, a ruthless Serbian policeman. It had its eyes watching and ears listening at all levels of the state including at the top of the Communist Party, whose members all had their phones tapped. They assumed this was by Tito and did not object. The civilian security service was itself being watched by its rival, the Croat-based military secret service.

If we had talked to our hosts, we would have been told that the Serbs dominated Yugoslavia from its inception, controlling the top government ministries and offices, the military's officer corps and the police. In 1929 the Serbian prince Aleksandr proclaimed a royal dictatorship.

We bypassed Bosnia, which was to our right. In 1950, a rebellion in Cazin against the collectivisation of agriculture and the centralised confiscation of produce was put down by the secret police whose officers were all Serbs, whilst the rebels were 90% Muslim. This was to be a foretaste of troubles ahead.

In Belgrade, capital of the Serbian republic, the atmosphere was much colder. Here we would have been told that in 1929, the Croats had set up an extremely radical, ultranationalist terrorist organisation the *Ustaše*, which forged close relations with the Italian and Hungarian fascists and, in 1934, assassinated King Alexsandr in Marseilles. As we didn't 'mention the war', we were not told that, following the German and Italian occupation in 1941, the *Ustaše* supported the Germans and set out to exterminate all the Serbs and Jews in Croatia by forcibly converting the former to Catholicism and deporting the latter to Hitler's gas chambers.

The *Ustaše* leader Ante Pavelic said about the Serbs, 'expel one-third, convert one-third and kill one-third.' The Nuremberg Tribunal described how 'the *Ustaše* offered to convert a village, so 250 villagers turned up, the church doors were locked, they were told to lie down and then six *Ustaše* beat them all to death with spiked clubs'. Mention Yugoslav history today to a Serb and his first word is *Ustaše*.

The Serbian nationalist guerrillas, the *Četniks*, however fought the Germans, but it was the Communist partisans led by Tito that were the most effective and gained the support of the British. The *Četniks* would later become the bogeymen for the Croats.

Tito, with an iron-fist, was now holding together these different people in a federation of six republics and two autonomous Serbian regions of non-Serbs, namely Vojvodina with its large Hungarian population and Kosovo with its Albanian majority. The three religions were dispersed: mainly Catholic in Slovenia and Croatia; mainly Orthodox in Serbia, Montenegro and Macedonia; and Muslim in Bosnia and Kosovo.

The scenery of the country varied from rolling hills in Slovenia through the vast plain of the river Sava in Croatia to the mountains of Serbia and Macedonia where the fields stretching into the distance formed a patchwork quilt. One evening we were camped in a valley south of Skopje, the capital of the Macedonian republic, and from the mountains above we heard the singing of a brigade of Young Communists building the *autoput*, the 'road of brotherhood and unity' according to Tito, though its two-lane construction would lead to many accidents.

Andrew, a traditional Conservative with his Austin-Healey 3000, was enchanted by socialist endeavour but not by socialist corruption at the border with Greece. By the time our adventure was over and we had seen the poverty of India, socialism had entered Andrew's life and became his guiding force.

Andrew was less enamoured by the youth with the Red Star on his shirt. Was this evidence of Soviet infiltration? In October 1944, Stalin and Churchill had agreed the percentage share each would have after the war:

Romania	Russia 90%	The others 10%
Greece	Britain 90%	Russia 10%
Yugoslavia	50–50%	
Hungary	50–50%	
Bulgaria	Russia 75%	The others 25%

After the war, Yugoslavia was part of a buffer zone of friendly Communist states set up to protect the Soviets from any future repeat of the German invasion, this time by the 'capitalist' West. This was the start of the Cold War.

Stalin ordered Tito to tone down his revolutionary zeal as he did not want to upset the agreement he had with Churchill and Roosevelt to a 50–50 share in the future of Yugoslavia: 'What's all this nonsense I hear about you wearing red stars in your caps? Form isn't important. What you achieve is important. And you prance around with – red stars! My God, the last thing we need is red stars!'

To control the friendly states Stalin set up the Cominform (Communist Information Bureau), with its headquarters in Belgrade. Tito mistook this as a Soviet favour and continued, without consulting Stalin, to support the Greek Communists. In June 1948, Stalin convened a meeting of Cominform, which condemned Tito and called on the Yugoslav Communists to either change their policies or change their government. Tito denounced the Soviets, and the other Cominform states severed their relations with Yugoslavia, which turned towards the West for assistance. This doomed the Greek Communists.

Yugoslavia with a population of 23 million had the fifth largest army in the world with 200,000 heavily armed conscripts, each with their own AK47, ready to fight against the Soviets. When the break up of Yugoslavia came in 1991, the weapons would be used in the fighting that followed.

CHAPTER 4
GREECE, OCCUPATION
AND CIVIL WAR

Saturday 7th July

Entry into Greece seemed to be coming from darkness into light. The officials were charming and as we drove the first few yards into Greece a soldier in national dress saluted us from the heights of his sentry box. The Italians we had met took us to Salonika where everyone was charming to us. We had our first experience of bartering and were given a free wash and brush up.

When we arrived we were yearning for a swim but the sight of garbage in the harbour was too much. John had his rucksack mended in the depth of a garage, the oxyacetylene lamp being the only light to illuminate what appeared to be the inquisitive faces of half the population of Salonika!

We waited in the terrible dust outside Salonika until picked up by a jeep and then a few miles out we were dropped and met a young boy who promised us a huge lift to Kavalla. An hour later the lorry turned up – driver obviously not pleased to see us. We went a quarter of the way to Kavalla, boy said goodbye and jumped off. Left alone with truck driver we prepared for long ride but after a few kilometres he turned off to quarry and we apprehensively felt for our knives as it was by now dark. No Kavalla after all. The boy by his uninhibited physical affection for us gave us our first taste of Eastern physical uninhibitedness. We slept the night in a river bed, quite good, beautiful evening. Soup and bread!

HITCHHIKING TO INDIA IN 1962

John's card from Salonika, Greece, Saturday

It is ... I had just started writing when along came two Persians and now I am 160 kilometres further on. It's hot. At least the rain is over. For 5 days we've had it. Now it's too hot! Yugoslavia is remarkable in its variance from the flat plains of Croatia to the patchwork quilt of Serbia and finally to the barren harsh beauty of the mountains of Macedonia. The Slovenes in the north and the Macedonians in the south are cheerful and friendly but otherwise our feelings have been blurred by the poverty. The communist system is a failure and one can only wait for the change. We are both fit and very smelly. Next address Tabriz, Iran. No letters yet. But we are ahead of schedule. All love, John.

Sunday 9th July

In Langadhikia, a toothy Greek military policeman insisted on having his photo taken with his beloved battered American bike.

The second lift took us from the middle of nowhere in an army jeep in which was being transported the local dead meat. Our rucksacks were put on top with the detriment of both meat and rucksacks.

Our next lift was to Kavalla with a big truck driver who was jovial enough to give us the benefit of his mournful rendering of a few Greek folk songs. We responded with 'Glory, glory, what a hell of a way to die'. We ate breakfast with him at a transport café – tomato salad, custard and bread. We had been picked up for this lift from the shelter of trees in the middle of nowhere and the comfort of two chairs provided by a kindly old lady. We lost a tent pole on this lift.

Our next lift after a bus ride out of Kavalla – of some

exhilaration, there being scarcely room to breathe. It being Sunday and us being by the sea we were surrounded on all sides by astonished bathers. However we had become hardened to this and waited patiently for our next lift – again a lorry. Very friendly couple in it. We stopped and they bought us beer, tomatoes and cheese, which we ate at the restaurant by the Aegean. I rode in the back of the lorry and had an exhilarating if rather hair-raising ride. We were left at a T-junction amongst a long and beautiful line of trees.

Now came our first hitch on a bus. We were taken free to Komitini! In Komitini we waited at another T-junction. The road signs towards Alexandropolis went both ways. The next bus which came along was forced to stop and take us due to the heroic exhortations of the local populace and local gendarme! The people on the bus were delightful. We were given collapsible seats and sat in the gangway. The man that John spoke to knew Ipswich Town were the best football side in England and had great respect for Arsenal! We were given sweets and cake by a very charming fat Greek woman who seemed to do it with more significance than most present givers. In the bus before we had been given pears. Once again I learned conversation was possible with the minimum of words.

We were dropped in Alexandropolis and saw the two Swedish girls who had been hitching – hardly Scandinavian beauties and suitcase denoted something more than hitchers. While waiting for lift, episode occurred with money changer. He offered us good exchange rate for £1 against Turkish lira. We did not know whether to trust him but eventually I took the plunge and followed him to a house in a side street where he took me up to the second floor of a suspiciously clinical type building. An old woman in black seemed to be expecting us and the whole time I was on tenderhooks waiting for a prearranged signal which would set in motion the means for my destruction – or what you will. In fact it turned out to be to our advantage. He gave us 31, Greek banks give 35 and Turkish banks give 25. We also met the most anti-English bicycle mender so we played him along while I pretended to be German.

We eventually got a lift out of town and were soon travelling fast through Greece towards the Turkish frontier. We were in the back of a lorry. The Aegean was on our right. The night above was perfect and all in all it was the most exhilarating lift we had. The driver drove fast but skilfully over the terrible road but no matter how well he avoided the potholes we were rattled unmercifully in the back. Eventually we started to pass through the last of the Greek villages on the way to the frontier and probably because it was Sunday, in every village we came across our headlights revealed throngs of people milling the road while the sidewalks too were packed with people drinking, talking and strolling. We seemed to notice that the men and women were often in separate groups. At one point we were held back by a wonderful herd of black goats and at the same point I have a clear recollection of my first and last Greek priest – square hat and beard – all in black.

Eventually we were left in a town just a few kilometres from the border. We got out and found ourselves in the middle of one of these crowded villages. We spent our last drachmas on beer and were soon the centrepiece of attraction for many of the local children who peered intently over our shoulders as we wrote our diaries. One or two of the adults came to talk to us. We noticed two men dancing together in the bar behind but there was nothing abnormal in this to the locals. Eventually we made our way to the end of the village and 'pitched camp' – slightly perturbed by the village dogs.

Monday 9th July

Up early – first lift in army jeep takes us to the border. On the way we join haphazard convoy with other jeeps and after much mock saluting and pidgin banter we arrived at the frontier.

John's thoughts on Greece

Greece was '*kali* this' and '*kalo* that'. In fact everything was '*ola kala*'. Only later did I realise that the Greek émigrés to America would introduce the shortened version 'OK' into their English language. Crossing the border from Yugoslavia where the customs had tried to send us back to Belgrade because it was suggested we were lacking a piece of paper, Andrew was much taken by the *Evzones* guard in his white pleated mini-skirt, his long woollen stockings and his boots with pompoms attached. He wasn't alone, and this trip started my lifelong love for Greece. Four years later, I returned. In *Greek Walls* I described this re-union:

'Nothing could have been better than the sight of Corfu as Jannie and I sailed on the Brindisi ferry through the Corfu Channel early on a June morning in 1966. To our left were the brown menacing mountains of Albania, on the right the gentle green of Corfu and ahead the silver mirage of the shimmering sea. Then out of the haze, slowly, magically, appeared Corfu Town with its magnificent buildings between two enormous forts. It was love at first sight.'

And this love is still very much alive as I write this book, overlooking the Ionian Sea in Corfu, where Jannie and I built a minute house in 1970 and raised our two children on holidays in the sun.

Greece in 1966 had serious problems – it was politically divided following German occupation and civil war. In my book *Greek Walls* I quoted from my mentor on Corfu, George Manessis:

'Greece is in a political crisis,' he said sadly. 'I fear the

Left is posing a real threat to the country's stability. Two and a half years ago, Greece elected a left-wing politician, Papandreou, as Prime Minister. Last year the king, who is your age, John, sacked him when he asked to be appointed Minister of National Defence. A general strike resulted, and now we have a complete breakdown of order. For eight years until 1963 we had an efficient Prime Minister, Konstantinos Karamanlis, who ran the country well. I wish he could be back in charge.'

'But George,' I countered, 'in England, two years ago, Labour took over from the Conservatives and we don't have chaos.'

'You cannot understand Greek politics until you understand Greek history. Only seventeen years ago the country was torn apart in a bitter four year civil war.' He pointed to the mountains on the mainland. 'Just over there, Greek fought Greek and hundreds of thousands were killed. When the Communists began to lose in 1948, they took away their children and transported them to the countries in Eastern Europe so that they would not fall under what they called the Fascists. Today, these children are your age. They are still separated from their families. Even though the Communist leaders have been exiled, they send orders from abroad to their cells in the country.'

To a simple-minded North European liberal, a country with king and parliament at odds, as well as the left and right fighting, plus a military force eager to intervene was all too baffling. Yet here we were, sitting in paradise, within a couple of miles of the Communist world – Albania, dark and ominous across the grey sea.

The military seized power in what they called 'the Revolution of 21st April 1967' to forestall a communist coup. No evidence was ever produced of such a plan. On 24th July 1974, Karamanlis was returned as Prime Minister. In May 1979, though the European Commission in Brussels doubted

GREECE, OCCUPATION AND CIVIL WAR

whether the economy and the inflated and cumbersome bureaucracy would allow the country to compete in the EEC, a treaty was signed admitting Greece as a full member from 1st January 1981.

The climax to my first visit to Greece occurred as we hitched a lift through Western Thrace with the Greek army up from Oriastada to the Turkish border towards Edirne. The young Greek conscripts – conscription is still in place today – were sublimely happy. At the sight of a young lady, the lads cheered in most unmilitary fashion. I later learnt this behaviour is called *kamaki*, which is a word used for spear fishing – shooting for the girls. As we passed through crowds promenading in the cool evening, music was weaving its magical charm – music that was not the Rock and Roll of the Beatles, but the wild folk tunes of Mikis Theodorakis that would hit the western ear just two years later with the launch of the film 'Zorba the Greek'. Men were dancing with men in Greek style, with arm stretched out over the next dancer's shoulder. The Greek way of life was converting this unromantic Northerner. Life seemed to be all happiness.

Western Thrace had been occupied by Bulgaria in the First World War but returned to Greece afterwards, but reoccupied in the Second World War, when the local Greeks rose up before 100,000 refugees fled into the German occupied zone around Salonika. Before the war, over 50,000 Jews lived in Salonika, making it one of the oldest Jewish communities in Europe, a community at peace with its Greek neighbours. Tragically, few countries in Europe lost a higher proportion of their Jewish population in Hitler's Final Solution than Greece. The Auschwitz camp commandant claimed that 60-65,000 Jews were brought from Greece. He told Adolf Eichmann that 'the Greek Jews were of such poor quality that all had to be eliminated'. By September 1944 only 2,469 were alive, and even fewer when the camp was liberated in January 1945.

The personal costs of the war in Greece were immense: the elimination of the Jews; the 250,000 people that died directly or indirectly as a result of the famine between 1941 and 1943; and the anti-guerrilla campaigns of 1943–44 when villages were wiped out as acts of revenge, such as that in Kalavryta in the Peloponnese, when 511 men were killed. It was also the economic cost to the Greeks that turned the Greeks against the Germans. In July 1942, with payments to Germany rising each month, Mussolini visited Athens and wrote to Hitler: 'Greece is on the brink of financial – and therefore economic and political – catastrophe'. Hitler did nothing but recommend that 'occupation costs' should be renamed 'construction costs'. This was followed by a mission to Germany by the Finance Minister. It was a total failure as no Greek politician carried enough weight to be heard seriously in Berlin. Hermann Goering put it succinctly: 'We cannot worry too much about starvation among the Greeks. Perhaps it is as well that it should be so, for certain nations must be decimated. But even if were not so, nothing could be done about it.'

German and Italian occupation, the latter in Corfu, in Greece led to a resistance movement. The strongest element of which were ELAS, the Communists.

In October 1944, Churchill had secretly agreed with Stalin in Moscow that 'we would have 90% say in Greece'. Stalin then sent a military mission to Greece, which told the Communists to face geopolitical realities and co-operate with the British. On Christmas Eve Churchill and Anthony Eden, determined to stop a Communist takeover, travelled to Athens, where they met Archbishop Damaskinos, whom Churchill came to admire, having previously described him as a 'pestilent priest, a survival from the Middle Ages'. Two weeks later ELAS and the British forces arranged a ceasefire.

Stalin did keep his word and did not support the Communists. It would have been difficult for him to do so, as the Soviet Union did not have access to the Mediterranean and probably more importantly Stalin knew he could use the Greek precedent when after the war he set up the buffer zone of Communist states in East Europe. He also knew that the Cold War would have turned into a hot war. By 1948, with Britain having serious financial problems, the USA had taken over against the Communists and he was fearful of another invasion of his homeland. As Stalin simply put the case, 'The Greek rebellion has not the slightest chance of victory. Do you really imagine that Britain and the United States – the strongest countries in the world – will tolerate any disruption to their communications artery in the Mediterranean! What rubbish. And we don't have a fleet. No – the rebellion in Greece must be crushed and the sooner, the better.'

After the war and the Axis defeat, the Communists fought on against the elected government leading to the Civil War which ended in 1949. In the Greek mountains from Western Thrace in the east, through Macedonia, where the guerrillas were strongest, to the Pindos in the west, Greeks killed Greeks. Over the 5 years of civil war at least 60,000 Greeks were killed. On top of this, more than 50,000 Greek speakers were refugees, many to Communist Yugoslavia.

At the end of the civil wars in Spain and Yugoslavia, many on the losing side were executed. In Greece the regime was far more lenient and the execution of political prisoners ceased when the fighting ceased although nearly 3,000 were still under sentence of death. Few of these in the end were executed.

The exodus from Greece continued in the 1960s; there was no work and little food in Greece. I have a friend, Anna, from Thrace whose father went to work as a *Gastarbeiter* or 'guest worker' in Germany, where there was a shortage of workers after the war. Her mother followed to set up home in Stuttgart so Anna lived with her grandparents. She followed in 1970, following in reverse the route we had hitchhiked.

Her grandfather was born in 1895 and owned sheep and cows. He fought the Turks and also the bears. After drinking a lot of ouzo he would dance with a bear. As children, they didn't think of the Turks as any different from themselves. An aunt spoke Turkish and they would sometimes travel to Edirne in Turkey, where goods were cheaper.

There is a personal, improvised Thracian dance, the Zeibekiko, which was originally taken from Western Thrace to Western Anatolia by the Zeybek Muslims and brought back to Western Thrace by the Christian refugees in 1922. Anna tells me the dancer bodily expresses defeat, despair of life, the complaint of the soul and an unfilled dream. The real man is not ashamed to manifest his pain; he improvises humbly and with dignity. The dance symbolises the tragedy of the *Megali Idea*, which I deal with at the end of the next chapter.

These days improvisation has been extended for the tourists' pleasure, with feats such as the dancer picking up a table by his teeth being performed.

CHAPTER 5
ISTANBUL, TURKS AND GREEKS

Monday 9th July

We walk from customs house to customs house. The Turks seemed a little firmer and less laisser-faire. However, we were somewhat distracted from this by the offer of a lift to Tehran by a German. Unfortunately our hopes were too highly raised. We left the customs elated and because of the lack of traffic started to walk to the nearest village. On the way we came across an old farmer and his boy irrigating their crops. They let us have a wash in the clear, refreshing water and then gave us some onions. Met two hitchers from Birmingham.

Started to walk again but were picked up by a German called Kroneder, who took us to Edirne and showed us a mosque there. No shoes, very beautiful. Wonderful impression of space given by the enormous dome and whole floor covered with every believable type of carpet. At each end the biggest chandelier I have ever seen and in the same part of the church was the altar, a magnificent erection consisting of a leather door and a flight of very steep steps leading to the priest's throne at the top. In the middle of the mosque was a table raised a long way off the ground.

At the local bazaar I went off to make a few pathetic attempts at bartering, while John hitched. We eventually ate some delicious cheese and bread sitting on the pavement at the side of the road. It seemed this attracted as much attention and interest as it had in other countries for we were soon approached by a couple of students with a little working knowledge of English.

We got a lift fairly soon on a fantastic Intercontinental Transport lorry driven by a real man. He shot his gun out of the window, played the wireless ear-splittingly loud and acted big in every way. We stopped a couple of times for drinks on the desolate 154-mile journey to Istanbul. There seemed to be hundreds and hundreds of fields under the burning sun but very few dwellings. One appreciated the dependence on water. The last stop but one our driver made was to clean his truck. This took about half an hour and eventually he hardly allowed us in the cabin with boots on so proud was he of his work. We conked out very soon after and there was another delay while he fixed various knocking noises in the engine. In fact we considered if we were ever going to get to Istanbul at all! When we arrived we had the parting shot – he asked us for some money. We refused of course.

We boarded a bus and fortunately came across some very charming Turks who gave us the name of a student hostel quite near the Hilton – this seemed to suit us very well. We arrived and were greeted by a really sinister looking Turk with very thick horn-rimmed spectacles. He had sleek, oily black hair and rather a stooping walk although he in fact was quite tall.

The most marked feature of this collection of little dormitories was the smell of urine. In fact the whole place was a contradiction in atmospheres, from the modern office of the director and the well-furnished sitting room to the dirty bedroom and filthy lavatory.

We went to eat in the restaurant on the basement floor, which served not only for students but also for passers-by in the street. At dinner, which (like all food in Istanbul) was very cheap, we met a charming young Turkish student. Although we were both very tired, we went for a long walk with him.

By far the most interesting thing he showed us was the street of whores. This was a side street joining two larger

ISTANBUL, TURKS AND GREEKS

side streets. Both ends were screened off so that one had to go in to see. The street consisted of about 100 houses, 50 down each side – all brothels and in each there were approximately 6 prostitutes selling themselves at 10 lira (35p) a time. Half of this went to the owner of the house who is always very wealthy, the other to the girls. All the girls, unless they were in action, exhibit themselves either in the doorways suitably undressed or if they have more confidence in the windows. The street was very crowded and although they were for the most part ugly the few attractive ones were kept busy the whole time giving their five minutes worth.

We took a walk down the main street, which leads from Taksim, and admired the fine shops. There were many people and this combined with the tremendous noise from the road works created an impression of great fervour and excitement.

On the way back we talked a lot. The most interesting thing he had to say was in connection with the pure Turkish race – Hitler's pure Aryan race – in fact the Turks are Aryan. The whole theory was frightening with its racialist ardour. He knew the whereabouts of all the fine Turkish stock in the world. He said Turkey needed a dictator more than anything else.

Religiously, the educated Turks seemed to have reached the same questioning stage that we have. The poor of course follow the Islam religion blindly with little understanding of its meaning.

Tuesday 10th July

Up quite late. Washed clothes, washed selves. We ate in pleasant restaurant and had remarkably cheap (considering the quality) meal.

On Tuesday evening John stayed in bed and I went out with our German friend Krommeder and our Turkish friend 'Flame' and a Dutch boy. A Turkish boy and a German girl – very artistic but a little mad – terrible capacity for senseless laughter and of course great verbosity. We went in Krommeder's Mercedes to a 3rd class restaurant somewhere in Istanbul, where the owner, fat man Mustafa, gave us some dried fish – very good – a little like meat.

We drank quite a lot. At one time there were about 25 bottles of beer on the table. After a while obscenities became prominent and one of the waiters kept trying to tickle Krommeder at the same time as making crude gestures with fingers and thumb – meaning come and suck my dick or go to hell. The atmosphere became warmer and warmer and more and more spontaneous as time went on. Every now and then a strong character would drift into the bar to be greeted hospitably by Mustafa or his friend.

Eventually we left and on the way back Flame told me about his sexual habits. He had a woman three nights before and this seemed a regular occurrence. Although the brothels were legal, above board and government inspected, there is a law in Turkey against intercourse before marriage.

When I got back to the dormitory John told me had 'gippo' tummy. And I didn't really worry too much.

John's card from Istanbul, Turkey, Tuesday

Hitching is over for a couple of days whilst we eat exotic dishes and sample adventures in this sordid city. Last night visited the street of prostitutes – a row of 50 houses – six whores in each. It is very sad and they were all pretty foul. At 6/- (30p) for 5 minutes neither customer nor producer gains much. Then great discussion with young Turkish student that lasted into the night. He was one of the young men who instigated the overthrow of Menderes. The Turks are a wild lot. Yesterday our last lift was in a huge lorry. The giant who was driving it produced a Hauser pistol and proceeded to shoot at sheep whilst we were travelling at 60 m.p.h. At the end of our journey with him he demanded money for kindness! Needless to say he received only an amused smirk from us two bums. We are staying in a cheap dormitory and moving on towards Persia in a few days. As we are ahead of schedule things look rosy for India. But Asia – just over the Bosphorus from here – might not be so kind to us. Still no news from home or Denmark. All love John.

Wednesday 11th July

Woke and saw John standing in the doorway, looking as though he had just seen a ghost – the porter! John was obviously a case of Gippo.

We travelled in a dolmuş (minibus) and were so sure at the end of the ride that we had been cheated that we jumped out having only paid quarter of the fare. From that time on we discarded our colourful and conspicuous hats. We also had John's camera mended in a highly suspicious office 5 floors up off the crowded main street. We were surprised to find the office there when we got back! The camera had been mended very well.

We then went to get the haversack mended and a new tube for the camp bed. This took us towards the Galata Bridge area, a teeming, over-populated, under-fed district where one sees all conceivable types of street-seller and porter. There was one whole road where the shops all sold the same kind of electrical piping. We had the haversack mended in an alley off a tiny steep-sided street sloping down towards the river. The jobs were very well done although we had to make sure we knew where to find the workshop in amongst the countless back streets.

When we went to post a lot of letters we met a man in the

Post Office who spoke very good English – he said he had self-taught in a year! He had had great trouble in getting a visa to leave Turkey to work in England. He said Turkey was a very sad country – 8 million unemployed. He worked in his uncle's barber shop and kindly told us to visit him whenever we felt like it.

By the time evening came round John's temperature had gone up to 102. We decided to go in the morning if John's temperature had gone down!

Thursday 12th July

Woke at 5.00 and looked down at John. He looked like death so I went back to sleep!

At 8.00 I phoned the doctor. Having tried a cabin in the road with no glass in the door and broken machinery I eventually phoned from a travel bureau that was being cleaned out before it opened.

The doctor came from the consulate and brought the pro-consul with him – very kind. He diagnosed dysentery, charged 40 lira, prescribed some medicine and left. Spent most of the rest of the day nursing the patient, attempting to get boiled rice, rather than greasy pilau. Although charming, the buffet workers seemed unable to understand we had a patient on our hands.

Another card from Istanbul, Thursday

I write this in order to get sympathy. I have contracted gypo tum – a severe form of diarrhoea – or whatever it is. The trouble has been caused by my tongue liking cucumbers but my stomach not. Tomorrow we leave for Ankara and unfortunately it will have to be by use of thumb alone. All our wangles have fallen through and so it will be a continuation of our adventures that will bring us to India. The next stage is 1,800 miles from Istanbul to Tehran (Iran). We hope we can do it in a week but perhaps we are optimistic. To get on the road again is the greatest thought at the moment and leaving Istanbul will not break either of our hearts. I hope little old you is having a sunny time on the Skaw. At times like this with no stationery I find I miss you a lot and the wait until October seems a long one. Look after yourself, your John.

Friday 13th July

John confined to bed but better so I decided to be a tourist for the afternoon.

Went off to visit Aya Sophia – supposed to be one of the greatest temples ever built. Unfortunately I arrived just as it was closing – 5.00.

As luck would have it there was an important temple just opposite called the Blue Mosque with some very beautiful tiling and fine stained glass. Once again the wonderful impression of space, the high pulpit with the Dunce's cap on top. The raised marble table on stone legs in the middle – obviously only used for ministerial convocations.

Although the interior was very impressive the low-slung elaborate lighting system did much to ruin the total effect. The exterior had the conventional dome and minarets and spacious courtyard – conventional except for the presence of 6 minarets (unique in the world), instead of the usual 4. It was the Mosque of the Sultan Ahmet.

From there to Istanbul's newest mosque at the head of the Galata Bridge. The first noticeable difference was the lack of colour – a dull brown stone as opposed to many blues and brightness of the other mosque. Secondly the great pillars (4 is the usual number for supporting the great dome) were rectangular rather than fluted in the Blue Mosque. They retained their impressiveness but lacked the grace that even such enormous pillars can possess.

The Egyptian Bazaar was the next tourist attraction and seemed to characterise much of the excitement of Istanbul. Everything conceivable was sold amid the maze of narrow tortuous streets where canopies stretching out from opposite shops practically met in the middle, obscuring the evening sun. Tramps buying rags. Everything sold. Went to mosque on top of the same hill. Hovels and slums all around Bazaar.

Saturday 14th July

John much better. Decided on trip down the Bosphorus. Ship left from Galata. On way across bridge, John wanted to buy some fried fish and bread being sold with great gusto off the many rowing boats precariously tossing in the choppy water at the quayside. Doctor said no!

We got boat to last stopping point before the Black Sea. It was a very pleasant trip although the outgoing journey was a little spoilt by the overcast weather and the presence of Turkish family whose son could speak a little English and was determined to take the opportunity of practising it. He persisted in a very determined way and we both took a dislike to him. We also met Turk who was very helpful but perhaps a little offended when John showed him money-belt.

At last point – very pretty little wooden houses with many colours. John had fish. I had swim – almost in the Black Sea! Coming back very beautiful.

Say goodbye to amusing French student in Harbya.

John's thoughts on Turks and Greeks

On the other side of the border from Oriastada, we joined the Turkish Army. We sat with stern-faced boys, probably peasants from Anatolia, whose mission was to prevent another Greek adventure. For us their puritanical view of the fairer sex was mystifying. Their tough appearance hid a welcoming nature based on the Islamic faith, which called for hospitality being given by the host to their guest. Reading Andrew's diaries again, I notice sex and hospitality is repeated frequently.

Other than feasting on fried fish on Galata Bridge, Istanbul was a disappointment for me, and a pleasure for Andrew. Laid up with dysentery, I had to listen to Andrew's stories of the Street of a Thousand Women.

I had time to ask myself a question. Why did the Greeks and Turks hate each other? Why were they determined to defend their countries by military means as they had shown on the border between Oriastada and Edirne?

1453 is a year etched on the heart of every Greek – the year Constantinople fell to the Ottomans. On Tuesday 29th May, the final vestige of the over one-thousand-year-old Christian Eastern Roman Empire was ended. Tuesday is still an unlucky day for the Greeks. The Ottomans then needed to create legal and administrative institutions for their non-Muslim subjects, who were now in the majority, and not governed by the Muslims' *Seriat*. In the following year, the *millet* (nations) system, based on the subject's religion, was introduced. The three *millets* were for the Orthodox Christians, with their patriarch in Constantinople, the Jews and an elected official of the rabbinical council at its head, and the Armenian Gregorian Christians, whose patriarch was also responsible for the Roman Catholics.

The Ottomans were respectful of the other 'Peoples of the Book', welcoming for example, the huge Sephardic Jewish population after their expulsion from the Iberian peninsular in 1492. A great number of these settled in Salonika, which we had just passed through, though few survived the forced transfer to the gas chambers of Hitler's Holocaust. I could therefore discount ancient hate. This led me to Greek's War of Independence in 1830 – some 130 years before. Of course there was slaughter on both sides – that's what happens when a people fight for the independence. I move on to the Balkan Wars of 1912 and 1913, when the Ottomans lost all the European part of their empire except Eastern Thrace. Again there would have been cruelty by Greeks and Turks but also by Serbians, Bulgarians and Albanians.

Anna from Oriastada suggested that for centuries the Christian peasants in the Ottoman Empire did not trust their feudal master, the *effendi* or 'lord', to whom they were obliged to render labour services. The equivalent is *efendikos* or boss in Greek. They also had to pay a poll tax or *haraç*. However, lack of trust is not hate. Other Greeks who know Thrace say that today the Muslims of Xanthi and Komotini, who remained in Greece after the great exchange of population in 1922, get on fine with their Christian neighbours. I therefore concluded that there must have been a trigger that created the hate.

Before and after Independence, the Greeks had played an important role in the Ottoman Empire. Their language was widely spoken throughout the empire, partially due to their strength in trading and their maritime skills. They had senior roles in Constantinople where they acted as translators for the Porte, the Ottoman Government.

In 1844, Ioannis Kolettis, a Hellenised Vlach, coined the slogan *Megali Idea* or Big Idea. He argued in Parliament, that there were two main centres of Hellenism: Athens, the capital of the new Kingdom of Greece, and the 'City' of Constantinople, 'the dream and hope of all Greeks'. He said: 'The Greek kingdom is not the whole of Greece, but only a part, the smallest and poorest part. A native is not only someone who lives within this Kingdom but also one who lives in Ioannina, in Thessaly, in Serres, in Adrianople, in Constantinople, in Trebizond, in Crete, in Samos and in

ISTANBUL, TURKS AND GREEKS

any land associated with Greek history or the Greek race.'

By the end of the Balkan Wars in July 1913, only Adrianople, which would be later renamed Edirne, Trebizond on the Black Sea and of course, Constantinople, by now Istanbul, were outside the Greek state. Anyway, an idea is usually just an idea. But this 'Big Idea' had far greater implications, and it wasn't just the Greeks that were pursuing the 'Idea'.

On 10th November 1912, Britain's Chancellor of the Exchequer David Lloyd George was entertaining the Greek consul in London and proposed a toast: 'I drink to the success of the Allies, the representative of one of whom we have here tonight, and may the Turk be turned out of Europe and sent to . . . where he came from.' The expletive has been lost to history. He added: 'Personally, I don't want him to keep Constantinople.' He also praised the fighting qualities of the Greek army.

A few weeks later Lloyd George met the Greek Prime Minister, Eleftherios Venizelos, whose single passion, having kicked the Turks out of his native Crete, was indeed the *Megali Idea*. *Eleftherios* is Greek for freedom. Lloyd George suggested that each country should be able to 'call on the other in case of difficulties or war'.

The Times praised 'the ablest of Greek statesman', stating that his vision of creating a mighty Greek empire in Asia Minor was breathtaking in scope and touched with genius. 'Large, bold and eminently practical, it pays homage to the exalted aspirations of Hellas, while it bears steadily in mind the most urgent and obvious of her material interests.' No one could be in any doubt, not least the Sultan in Constantinople, that the *Megali Idea* implied the dismemberment of the Ottoman Empire.

In the First World War, Venizelos, as Prime Minister, wanted to join the allies in the landing at Gallipoli in exchange for extensive territorial gains in Asia Minor.

Colonel Ioannis Metaxas, who would later become dictator of Greece and national hero when he said 'No!' to letting the Italians into the country in 1941, spelt out the implications in two memoranda to Venizelos: 'The Greeks almost all lived on the coastal periphery of Anatolia and since a large proportion worked as merchants or professionals, they offered a very poor social and geographic base from which to wage a war of expansion. The Moslems, numbering about seven million, not only occupied the whole of the Central Anatolian plateau in a compact mass, but also outnumbered the Greeks in most of the coastal districts ... The bulk of the Moslem population was composed of peasants, inured to the use of arms, whereas the contrary was the case with the Greeks. Above all, the military challenge could never be met, as the Turkish army would always be able to lure the Greek forces into the interior, an operation that the Greek army could not sustain. In other words, Napoleon's experience of 1812, when he invaded Russia, would be repeated again.'

Venizelos was overruled by King Constantine who, though initially in favour, preferred 'a small but honourable Greece'. This led to the great 'National Schism', which lasted for 30 years. I therefore rejected the First World War as the reason for the hate between Turks and the Greeks.

Venizelos's wish to regain their Byzantine Empire came true in 1919 at the Peace Conference in Paris when the victorious powers of France and America supported Lloyd George in asking the Greeks to occupy the Ottoman port of Smyrna, Islam's City of Tolerance, before the Italians could get there.

Tragically the Greeks, landing 13,000 troops on May 15th, committed atrocities by the end of the day. Initially, overcome by the emotion of returning to the Asian mainland, the troops stacked their rifles in a great pile on the quayside and then, to the pleasure of the cheering Greek community, performed Greek dances around it.

The elite *Evzones* regiment, who should have disembarked between the Greek and Turkish quarters to prevent future disturbances, arrived at the centre of the quay, where they were met by the Metropolitan who, after blessing them, led the troops and the crowd along the quayside.

A single shot from the Turkish quarter was met by a twenty-five-minute-barrage from the *Evzones*, mainly targeted at the Turkish garrison, which surrendered. The Turks, many beaten on the way, were led back to a Greek ship as prisoners of war. Many of the Greek troops then went on the rampage. That evening, after a torrential downpour, between 300 and 500 mainly Turkish corpses lay on the ground, where they were set upon by the Greek population and troops and stripped of their belongings.

This single act was perhaps the trigger that started the hate between the Turks and the Greeks. In the next three years the Greek Army captured 60,000 square miles of North West Anatolia, right up the Sea of Marmara across from Constantinople, which was now being occupied by the British.

The hate was completed when, in September 1922, the Turks under Mustafa Kemal (soon to be Atatürk), fought their way back to the Aegean coast and defeated the great Greek Army. On their arrival there, they gained their revenge for the humiliation in 1919 by fearful rape and pillage ending in the burning of the cosmopolitan heaven of Smyrna, when they recaptured the great city. Up to 30,000 Greek and Armenian Christians perished.

The British who had promised to support the Greeks, and the French, the Americans and the Italians, in their great warships in the bay evacuated their own citizens, but just watched as the inferno devoured the city. Only by the individual courage of an American working for the local YMCA were the onlookers made to come to the rescue of the mass of people who were on the quayside. Eventually with support from a flotilla from the nearby Greek island of Mytilene, some 150,000 to 200,000 Greeks were evacuated. Probably 30,000 able-bodied Greek and Armenian men were marched into the interior of Anatolia to a fate unknown.

At the peace conference in Lausanne in 1923, it was agreed that 1.3 million Christians, both ethnic Greeks and Turks, were to be expelled from the new Turkey in exchange for 480,000 Muslims that had to leave Greece, though over 100,000 Turkish-speaking Muslims stayed in Western Thrace and slightly more Greeks remained in Constantinople, though perhaps only 2,500 still live there today.

For the Greeks, the Great Idea had become the Catastrophe. For Lloyd George, who had underestimated Atatürk by calling him a 'carpet seller in a bazaar', it led to his sacking as Prime Minister. Perhaps the only good thing that came out of this tragedy was that Greece, as a country, became the most homogenous in the Balkans.

CHAPTER 6
TURKEY AND ARMENIANS

Sunday 15th July

Up at 5.30 and took taxi down to ferry. Managed to barter from 5 to 4 lira! At ferry got Vauxhall with charming couple.

Second lift in big American car with happy character in back. Once more pidgin Turkish came in useful.

Arrived Ankara quite late. Saw tomb of Atatürk up on the hill – very impressive classical Greek style. Ankara seemed to have none of the character of Istanbul – a symbolic rather than real capital.

Trouble with John's passport. Left at post office – rushed back before it closed and taxi man profited from panic and took all John's money – 2.50 lira.

Met Swiss who although very knowledgeable and well travelled was a little too eager with his information, especially data on temperature etc. making out that trip was hardly worth making.

Met charming English soldier (half-Jamaican stationed in Cyprus) who showed us a restaurant and proceeded to buy us a meal.

Difficulty in getting out of Ankara – enormous signpost one way – we go the other! Still people paying for us and being very helpful. We had one lift and man offered to put us up for night but changed his mind when chauffeur refused to get up early in the morning! Eventually we got onto main road out of Ankara and camped near howling cats.

Monday 16th July

First lift lorry – very ramshackle and driven by debauched little Turk – rather seedy – very fast.

Next lift in lorry with iron bars in back – delightful trio in front, three generations – very fit and strong grandfather, father adoring grandson who was allowed to steer. Back axle broke going up hill and we took sad farewell from family as next lift came along.

In Kayseri lots of children – met doctor who spoke a little English. Then lift in truck driven by two Canadian teachers who were going to work in work camp.

Hitched the next lift – a long one to Sivas – in seconds. Got the car following. Driven by very kind Turk who enjoyed our singing. Three quarters of the way there two peasants got in – very poor and characteristically dressed.

Camped practically in Sivas but were not molested by humans – just mosquitos! Were nearly offered a night in police station – a pretty slapdash police station too.

However, preceding this was the eventful arrival in town. We were dropped outside hotel, saw German car outside and went in to talk them up – no luck! But after 5 minutes manager came up and insisted we eat on the house. We had an enormous meal and the courses seemed never-ending – the whole was washed down by tepid, nasty tasting white wine. One of the biggest meals ever – John had great shish kebab.

Tuesday 17th July

First lift in fast Jeep to really god-forsaken village. Before they left they bought us a couple of cups of tea. Always the kindness. We prepared for a long wait and were soon surrounded by children. One sweet 14 year old bought us another cup of tea and produced all her limited English

TURKEY AND ARMENIANS

vocabulary in one burst. John went up the nearest hill to write poetry. First we took photos – all the girls scattered – a sign of Eastern habits, and boys gathered to stand stock still before the camera.

After not too long our lift came – 11 ton truck carrying bulldozer going to Erzincan first day – incredibly slowly over beautiful mountain passes – the great mountainous area of most of Turkey, east of Ankara. We soon became friendly with 4 drivers and they seemed out of the ordinary run of lorry types. 2 had had quite extensive studies.

One we nicknamed Charlie Chaplin was a great character, mimic especially. His driving was not as good as the boss's who was more serious but every bit as good-natured. He knew a little English and made heroic attempts the whole afternoon at conversation. The strain on me was great – on him must have been enormous as every sentence took about 5 minutes each way to communicate.

The other two didn't drive – one like Marlon Brando spoke a little French and was just as keen on conversing and John and he had a very amusing conversation about Princess Anne who he was determined to marry! I promised the boss to fix him up with an English girl – photos etc.

They bought us lunch on the way – in fact they bought us everything. In return we sang and did our best to make them feel our company worthwhile. Arrived late evening in Erzincan and ate great meal. Had hottest pepper ever – tears to eyes. Tried good deal of Raki – Turkish Pernod – and went off for what was supposedly an hour's sleep before arriving Erzerum 6.00 in the morning.

Managed to arrange sacking comfortably under great shadow of bulldozer. Mosquitoes not too bad. Heard strange bird with far-carrying cry. Woke at 2.00 a.m. and suddenly realised that we were still in Erzincan. Perhaps they had meant 6.00 in the evening. Anyway, at 5.00 we moved off and remarkably enough managed to sleep very well until first stop at 7.00 for tea. We arrived Erzerum about 10.00 and left the best lift we had had yet.

Wednesday 18th July

Took bus through Erzerum and arrived outside little café. Lift with Englishman and new wife in 2cv to Ağri.

In Erzerum visited mosque. Turkish pride in monuments emerging. Arches in double rows – a little Gothic – with pointed arches. The Englishman did not seem to have accustomed himself to Turkish way of life. Asking boy why he kept jacket on when it was so hot. His disappointment that Turkish people were so non-material minded – that they only wanted enough to live on – non-mercenary. They were both teachers at Turkish school. They gave us fast ride to Ağri where we ate skimpy meal and were driven out of town to bridge.

More children – one part noisy and leading. Lift in truck – very fast to Doğubayazit. Found Mercedes and arranged for him to take us to Tabriz in morning. Settled down to camp night opposite Mount Ararat, in mosquito-infected area. Over dinner where they overcharged us and we spent out last Turkish money there were an amazing number of insects dropping into our food. We were nearly got out of bed in morning by a bull that had got out of control of its keeper who eventually had to run half a mile to catch it!

There were some sweet children who came to our site on the football pitch – but a little too inquisitive for comfort. They made amends by bringing us firewood and a couple of apricots just as we were going. Children are cruel though and teased the cat caught in the football net and nearly choking. We had tried to free it before but receiving some very nasty scratching. John left camera behind. *Un bon petit cadeau pour les enfants*!

Left about 9.00 in crowded car. Arrived customs and

TURKEY AND ARMENIANS

experienced wait worse than any before. No love lost between Turks and Iranians as they stand on either side of railing separating two countries. Met Persian with MG Sprite – useless and unscrupulous. Lives in Brighton and screws all the women around.

Met German who had lost wife and child 7 months back. Now wandering world, playing accordion. Lost all possessions when car caught fire in Istanbul. One realises what life can bring. Also one realises that not all the people we meet are doing the same as us and are maladjusted socially. Met ex-Cambridge couple living in Isfahan – girl a typical Newnham product – showing no signs of femininity at all and a disturbingly high degree of intellectualism. However they were very helpful – accused our English signs as being immoral – higher education for you!

We were feeling fairly contented at the border for while it was obvious that lifts were hard to come by we had the Turk who had brought us to the border waiting for us. Because of sleep, lunch breaks and general bloody-mindedness on the part of the Persian customs we learnt that he was not going till 7.00 in the evening. We prepared for long wait at same time as looking for lift. The heat was very great and the Iranian atmosphere a little oppressive and the beauty of Mount Ararat, rising up behind the Turkish customs, was rather lost on us. Eventually our man did the dirty on us and drove off with an empty car.

We now moved into action asking everyone. Most of them told us to take the bus, which was waiting to go and an obvious disadvantage as far as we were concerned. When it left we tried more hitching, had an expensive bowl of soup at 2/6 each in the tourist Iranian hotel and prepared for kip. Put beds up just by exit to customs in front of garage – quite hot and many bugs. Prepared to catch the 6.00 morning bus to Tabriz.

John's card from Dogubayazit, Turkey, 19th July

Dear old you. I feel a bit guilty not writing for so long but things have been happening. We are now at Ağri – the last outpost in Turkey before the Iranian frontier, which is still 75 miles away. Huge plain between high mountains. Mount Ararat is just down the road. As little traffic comes this way (7-a-day we are told) it might be a long wait. Since Istanbul lifts have been fantastic and it is now 2 days since we bought a meal. The people are so generous and most unlike the vicious head-hunting tribe I had been led to believe. How does this read: Instanbul to Ankara 290 miles Sunday; Ankara to Sivas 300 miles Monday; Sivas to here 500 miles in a day and a half and this is through stupendous scenery. Underneath a thick layer of dust is a faint tan and the whiskers are now uneven but still short. If I get a chance to post this some time this week I will! But life in the wilds of Turkey isn't very civilised. 2 buses a week on main road! Will arrive Tehran Friday, Isfahan Sunday so write Quetta Pakistan. All my love John.

John's thoughts on Turkey and the Armenians

Andrew during his expeditions in Istanbul, had met a young man who talked of the Turkish race as 'pure Aryan' and reminded Andrew of Hitler's language. Was this a forewarning of our entry into Armenian Turkey and its participation in a precursor to the great genocide of the Jewish race? Or was the Holocaust the sole attempt in human history to exterminate an entire people by industrialised means? Or was it a young man's mythical glorification of Turkish ethnic identity, a pillar on which the Young Turks built their desire for the restoration of Ottoman pride?

Memories of foreign lands are often summed up in the few words of the local language one pick up. The *'dobros'* and *'kalos'* of Yugoslavia and Greece were followed by five words in Turkish that I have used with great success ever since: *'Memnun oldum çok iyi yim'*. This courteous greeting summed up our relations with the Turks: 'It is with great pleasure that I meet you'. Riding in trucks had replaced lifts in cars; our hosts offered us small tokens of hospitality whenever we stopped. The great Asian landmass of Anatolia threw up magnificent sights from the high conical mountain beside Kayseri, perhaps some ancient volcano, to the bare plateau of Eastern Anatolia, with Erzerum, the gateway to Central Anatolia from the east, and finally the borderlands dominated by the 15,000-feet-high Mount Ararat, the symbol of the Armenian people.

It was as we entered Eastern Anatolia and Historic Armenia, after its first town of Sivas, that I recall my second life-changing experience. Climbing out of the river valley, I looked down on the total tranquillity of poplar trees rising up from a narrow strip of green following the twinkling river. I took out a piece of paper and wrote a poem. I wish I could retrieve that magical moment. I had never before written a poem nor even an essay. We mathematicians got by with our equations. Just as we had passed through Thrace with its history of population exchange, here now in Eastern Anatolia, we were passing through a place of massacres or even genocide. Was it fate that made me climb up the hill and experience a false impression of heaven?

If I had written prose rather than poetry, I might have made up a short story something like this.

* * * * * *

With the mountains all around and the valley in all its morning glory, how could Andrew call this a 'god forsaken village'? At that moment, I see a man climbing the hill towards me. He has a dog, one of those dogs my friend's father had on his farm below the Downs at Folkestone. One moment it rushes off, then at the command of its master it stops, turns and slowly moves ahead – a sheepdog for certain. The man stops and I call out:

'Memnun oldum çok iyi yim'.

He smiles and gabbling away in Turkish indicates he would like to sit down. That's the problem with saying five words in a foreign language – it's assumed I can speak it.

We sit in silence for a while.

I point to the river and the valley and suggest they are beautiful: '*Güzel*'.

He shrugs his shoulders and there is another long silence. '*Hristiyan?*'

'*Evet*'. Yes. I lie a little; few of us practice Christianity any more.

'*Ortodoks?*'

'*Hayir*'. I can do yes and no but little else.

'*Ermeni?*'

I deny I am an Armenian.

'*Misyoner?*' I'm not that either but I tell him my brother is a missionary. Well he and his wife bring bibles to Turkey, which I always think is suicidal. Jimmy explains that the Turks, like us, are 'People of the Book'. Anyway, it is his way of saying 'thank you' for hospitality.

There is another long silence so I ask him: '*Hristiyan?*'

His instant denial suggests he has never been one either. From which I infer he cannot be Armenian. Many Armenians converted in the First World War; it was a way to survive.

'*Müslüman?*'

'*Evet*'. I now have a problem. What type? He's in his early sixties and roughly dressed. He is probably on his way up into the mountains with his dog, so I guess he's a shepherd. Most people around here are Kurds and there are a few Circassians, who were deported from the Northern Caucasus. They are all Sunni. Something tells me he's neither.

'Alevi?' His huge smile tells me I have chosen well. This Shia sect has been persecuted for centuries, but unlike the Kurds at the top of the pile and the Armenians in the middle, the Alevi were at the bottom. They have never been wealthy and have never had great possessions.

I have opened the forbidden door, the door to the room full of secrets. I write '1915' on my note pad and show him the year when the massacres took place. I want to know how old he was so I use my hand to indicate baby, boy and man.

'*On* ... .' My Turkish numbers had reached ten, which was '*on*' so he must have been a teenager.

I salute and suggest he was in the army. He shakes his head and points to the mountains. Like many Alevis, Armenians and Kurds, he was a draft dodger, sensible fellow. In those days, and probably now, it was the job of the local police, the gendarme, to round them up and get them to the front. Deserters were not treated as kindly.

I point up the valley, where the river is running crystal-clear and then to the '1915' on my pad. I sweep my arm from where we are going to indicate people coming down the valley. '*Ermeni*? Erzerum?'

He corrects me: 'Erzincan.' That's the next town we will come to.

I point down the valley to where we have just been and to where the Armenians would have gone. 'Sivas?'

He nods. 'Kayseri?'

'*Hayir. Suriye.*'

I want to know how many Armenians came this way and on to Syria. I write on my pad '100'. He moves his hand upwards. It stops at '600'. I ask him how many gendarmes, because I had read that these caravans of deportees were guarded. I put out two hands for ten:

'*On?*'

He repeats this four times so there must have been forty gendarmes.

I raise my arm to pretend I am shooting.

He nods.

I salute to suggest I am in the Army.

'*Hayir. Rusya. Gelibolu.*' So it wasn't the Turkish Army doing the shooting, they were fighting on the Russian Front and at Gallipoli.

He pretends to ride a horse. '*Kürtler*'. So it was the Kurd cavalry who did the shooting.

Then everything came out in a lengthy charade. The Armenians had stopped to ford the river when they were ambushed. They fought with pitchforks, knives and clubs against the Kurds with their guns and their swords. The latter were obviously one of the local militia set up by the provincial Governor to control the area.

'Gendarme?'

He shrugs his shoulders. He raises his imaginary gun, so they were involved.

He is now angry and waves the imaginary sword and pretends to cut his throat. All the men, women and children were massacred. I query that all 600 are dead and he indicates a girl. I think he says the Kurds give her to the *şeyh*, the sheikh or clan leader. He then indicates they ransack the belonging of the refugees. He is very sad and gets up to continue his journey up into the mountains.

I point again to the clear river below and repeat that it is beautiful: '*Güzel*'.

'*Güzel*'. He shakes his head. '*Hayir. Kızıl*'.

Once he has left I take out my pocket dictionary and look up the word *Kızıl*.

The river was red – with the blood of Armenians!

[Later I read that, when Ahmet Aga, the Chief of the

TURKEY AND ARMENIANS

Kurdish Cibran clan, was offered ox-carts of booty, he said: 'If God is God of all the world, he will not forgive you for this.'

He was not alone in not being involved in the massacres.]

Andrew was right. This is a god-forsaken village.

* * * * * *

What more do we know about the deportation of the Armenians?

With the advent of the First World War, Turkey, under the rule of the Young Turks who had seized power from the Ottomans in 1908, were suffering on all fronts. The offensive of the Turkish Third Army in the Caucasus at the onset of war had ended in disastrous failure and crippling losses, and the Russian forces were advancing into Anatolia. The British had taken Basra and were moving towards Baghdad, and the Turkish attack on Egypt had been stopped at the Suez Canal. In April 1915, the Allied forces landed at Gallipoli. In May, there was a rebellion in the city of Van, south of Erzerum, which the Turks had to hand over to the Russians, who were assisted by Armenian fighters. According to American and German missionaries, Armenians had then for three days taken revenge on local Turks killing all males that they could find. The leader of the Armenian defence committee was then made governor of the region. Fearing the collapse of the Empire, and blaming the failures in Eastern Anatolia on the Armenians, the Young Turks decided on removing the Armenians from Anatolia to Syria, still part of Turkish Empire.

Though the decision was taken in Constantinople, its execution was delegated to the local officials, who were told that local gendarmes should accompany and protect the groups of deportees. The execution of these orders varied considerably. With every able-bodied man in the Army, the gendarme force resorted to emptying the prisons for recruits. Therefore some of the refugees were not protected but pillaged by the gendarmes. Twenty years before, the Kurdish militia had been set up to control the Armenians and, given the opportunity, they now attacked the columns of ox carts fully loaded with the Armenians' possessions. With the hatred built up over many years this led to the massacre of defenceless deportees, whose guns had already been confiscated.

The death toll varied according to the distance the columns had to travel to get to Syria and whether it was through areas populated by Kurds, a high number from Erzerum in north-east Anatolia, a smaller number from the Black Sea coast around Trabzon, where there were fewer Armenians, very few from Cilicia in south Anatolia near the Mediterranean; and almost none from Aleppo, Turkey's third largest city as the government had made an exemption order for the city. From the two major cities of Constantinople and Smyrna, there were no deportations.

Of those Armenians that eventually reached Syria many were held on the border in a transit camp at Ras-ul-Ain (now Sari Kani), some 250 miles north east of Aleppo, and were subject to massacres and pillage by local Circassians, whose houses were reported to be full of the belongings of Armenians. They then had to make their way mainly by foot across harsh deserts 125 miles to camps along the Euphrates River, and up to 250 miles to the south east of Aleppo. Water stations were every 40 miles or 3 days walk apart and many perished through lack of food and water. The lucky few might have taken the Baghdad Railway to the Euphrates and then travelled by boat to another transit camp at Maskanah, where tens of thousands died. Further down the Euphrates the transit camp at Ar Raqqah became a permanent resettlement camp with many deportees moving into the town. Some were moved on to build roads near Urfa 100 miles to the north. These received a daily ration of bread.

The final area for resettlement was in the camps or towns near Deir ez-Zur. In the first year of deportation perhaps up to 200,000 reached this area. It was here that most died with a daily death toll of between 150 and 200. Their troubles were not over as once the population of any camp exceeded the 10% of the area's total population the excess was moved on towards Mosul some 350 miles away. These were subject to further massacres by Kurds and Circassians and also Bedouin tribesmen.

A further 132,000 were resettled 400 miles away in southern Syria in the Damascus region, where work could be found in the cities of Hama, Homs and Damascus. These Armenians were not subject to massacres but 20,000 died from disease and starvation, which was gripping the whole Turkish population.

Over 600,000, over a third of the pre-war Turkish Armenian population, lost their lives.

Unlike the Jewish genocide, there was a background to the Massacres. This in no way excuses what happened.

In the 18th century there had been five Russian-Turkish wars; in the 19th there were a further four. Of these nine wars, the Ottomans had been victorious in only two, one of which was the Crimean War when Britain, France and Italy had been its allies. In 1877, Russia attacked the Ottomans in revenge for the atrocities carried out against fellow Orthodox Bulgarians who had risen in an attempt to gain independence. In 1878 Russia stopped on the outskirts of Constantinople. In the east, Russia, led by an Armenian general, captured Erzerum. The Ottoman Armenians, though probably sympathetic to their co-Christians, did little more than act as guides but, from being 'the most loyal *millet*', the Armenians now became suspected by the Sultan of being in league with a foreign power. On the withdrawal of the Russian troops following the Treaty of Berlin, the Sunni Kurds and Circassians, (half a million of whom had themselves been expelled from their North Caucasus homeland by the Russians in the 1860s), pillaged the unarmed Armenian villages, leading to thousands taking refuge across the border in Russia.

The Armenians responded to the failure of the western powers to enforce the protective provisions of the Treaty by organising a revolutionary movement, which harassed the Ottomans. They could see that the Bulgarians in the west had gained their independence but the Armenians in the east were still under the Ottoman yoke. The programme of one revolutionary party stated: 'The time for the general revolution in Armenia will be when a foreign power attacks Turkey externally. The party shall revolt internally.' The Sultan learnt of this programme and set up Kurdish militias to suppress the Armenians. In 1894 Armenian villagers, under the prodding of the revolutionaries, refused to pay their customary tribute to the Kurdish chiefs. This led to the massacres of 1894 to 1896, when tens of thousands of Armenians were killed, many by the Muslim Kurds but also by the Muslim Circassians.

Andrew in his diary summed up his thoughts: 'Sun was setting behind the great mountain ranges all around Mount Ararat on the right. There was the wonderful strength of nature and the insignificance of man.' Only later did we understand the history of this tragic part of the world.

By now, team responsibilities had been assigned. I was to read the map to make sure we were going to India and also to get the lifts. Andrew would sit with the driver and attempt to communicate. He learnt Greek and Persian, whilst I tried my hand at Turkish

My job was complicated by the willingness of the locals to help us on our way. Whenever we were dropped off from a lift, a crowd of boys would gather and I would state the next town on our journey. Directions would be suggested and off we would stagger under the weight of huge rucksacks towards the road out of town. I found it essential to check that we were actually on the right route, so I would ask the next bystander for directions. Frequently these directions would contradict the previous suggestions. In the end we decided a democratic approach was best. Once we had reached a substantial majority in a particular direction, we would accept the collective wisdom of our helpers.

New challenges awaited us at the Turkish-Iranian border after Dogubayazit. Andrew was deep into his Persian phrase book and I went in search of a lift. Having learnt: *dobro*, *kalo* and *iyi*, which is Turkish for good, he announced that all we needed was '*khoob*' and '*na khoob*'.

I was to disappoint him. Amongst the truck drivers waiting to clear customs, there were a couple of what I guessed were Indians. Their language reminded me of the curry houses at home. I rolled my arm over in the action of a spin-bowler and they grinned. They were from Pakistan. England had just won the first three test matches against Pakistan but there was more important business to discuss. With great charm and perhaps some concern, they agreed to take us to Tehran. Their gesture confirmed a theory I was formulating: the further east one travelled, the more friendly and hospitable were the locals.

CHAPTER 7
IRAN TO TEHRAN AFTER
THE CIA COUP

Friday 20th July

4.10 a.m. John woke and saw two people on top of bus – a few minutes later it was gone. I had made lethargic effort to take in situation but had been signalled back to bed by bystander. No second bidding was needed!

We had some breakfast with the English couple and then John noticed some Pakistanis had arrived – 2 in a car each. He went out and bowled an imaginary cricket ball to the taller of the two. The ball was returned and a lift reluctantly conceded. We set off, John with Afiki, the big one in an Opel and myself with the lesser character Mukta in a Fiat. We set off for Tabriz about 11.00 and soon encountered the appalling road conditions, which were to shake us for the next 600 miles. Both cars were new and every bump was felt by the drivers.

Almost as soon as we were in Iran an impressive and dramatic change occurred in the landscape. From moderately cultivated land even in the remotest parts, we came across enormous expanses of semi-desert. The only thing relieving the monotony of the brown was the arid green scrub. We saw our first camels – strong one-humped beasts looking entirely capable of the hard life allotted them in nature's hierarchy.

The road taking us across this inferno is the only one into Persia from Turkey. It was much more than the adjective corrugated implies. Constant deep ruts not only jarred the car but also dragged it backwards. In addition there was dust the whole time and every time we were passed either way vigorous window-winding operations had to take place.

We arrived in Tabriz early evening and started to look for a hotel. Afiki and Mukta booked in and we took advantage by having a good wash down in the hotel courtyard. We left for a meal and were picked up by a Persian boy – obviously the Tabriz ambassador – who showed us the post office and then a restaurant where he allowed us to buy him a meal. Our shorts made a great hit and were laughed at everywhere.

We went back to the hotel and were poured a large whisky while Afiki showed us some of the qualities that had caused his promotion to Major in CENTO. He was being asked by the hotel manager to report to the police station and have his passport stamped. He naturally refused and in a very cool and forceful way fought off the pleas and threats of most of the hotel administrative staff until finally he decided to leave rather than break his principle. We then went to watch them eat in the best hotel in town – very interesting meal: rice, kebab, tomatoes, beans and potatoes (chipped).

Before then a 2cv had arrived in town to be immediately surrounded by a large male crowd out for a bit of inquisitive fun. Unfortunately they started playing with the cars and their attentions, if not hostile, were not harmless. We left Tabriz quite late and after 30 miles on a terrible road we stopped for a kip. Afiki and Mukta in the Fiat and us on beds. Sleeping too close to road for my comfort.

Saturday 21st July

At 4.30 we got up and found some wood and made the others a cup of witch's brew tea. At about 5.30 we set off on the worst day's motoring I've ever experienced. Apart from dust and corrugations, the very fast buses often driving us into the side of the road were an added menace.

By the end of the day sleep threatened to overcome both

drivers and Afiki had several fits of vertigo. We travelled on all the time even through the heat of the day reaching Tehran at about 11 p.m., mercifully having spent the last 100 miles on pretty good tarmac, although the Persian night driving was bad enough, no dippers for headlights.

Arrived Tehran, after much misdirection we found hotel for Pakistanis. We then started to look for one we had been recommended – both very irritable and exhausted – no luck. Eventually met man, who from balcony shouted down name 'Cyrus'. Met another man who had offered us free taxi ride to 'Tourist' – ugh hotel. Could not find hotel but then took me by the hand and showed me where it was. Got manager out of bed in pants at 1.00, paid 10/- each for what looked pretty reasonable. Upstairs found we were sleeping next to what looked very much like a tart. She locked her door after encouraging opening conversation and John's knocking was unanswered.

Sunday 22nd July

Up at about 9.00 – shower (shit, shave, shampoo, shag) and John bought great breakfast for nothing: pancakes – Persian bread, lemon and sugar, bottle of milk and watermelon. Sent postcards and fell asleep from 12.00 to 4.00 – very tired. Afiki lift had not materialised so we had to start hitching again.

We eat and take taxi to the exit from town. Arrived at nightfall at crowded crossroads at one of the exits from Tehran. Soon surrounded by a number of locals – not entirely friendly. After while I was told where we could find 'machines' and went off leaving John to experience very nasty few minutes with large crowd of men who threatened any minute to whip all the stuff. He had to leave a policeman to guard it while moving away.

John's thoughts on Iran's CIA Coup

Iran was for us a new world yet an ancient civilisation. Nine years later the Shah of Shahs would celebrate 2,500 years of the Persian monarchy at Persepolis. It would showcase the great advances it had made towards a modern industrial nation. Our first impressions were less than enthusiastic. For hundreds of miles we travelled over corrugated roads. A few hours before we arrived in Tehran we learnt of a major earthquake at Bou'in-Zahra, not far off the main road. This killed 12,000 people. A national appeal for help had gone out, so we donated our camp beds and sleeping bags. We at last could travel light.

Our Pakistani friends drove through Tehran to drop us off on the road to Isfahan. This typical kindness would be matched from now on: directions would no longer be given. Instead our guide would accompany us to where we wanted to go. Our first impression of Tehran was positive. Andrew, with his fluent Farsi, went off in search of lunch, flat bread and lemon to provide a perfect pancake. We already had a jar of sugar. He returned from his shopping trip hand in hand with his guide. It seemed to be the natural behaviour of Iranian friends.

On another expedition to buy something, Andrew had left me as custodian of the rucksacks and planner of the trip. I had gathered a larger group of boys and young men. They jabbered away at me in their foreign language. All I could muster in response was: '*Pool nadoram*', 'I have no money'.

What happened next was my third life-changing experience. By now the mob, to which had been added a few rough-necks had become angry, perhaps life-threatening as Andrew suggests in his diary. A few insults were being thrown and suddenly I caught a word I understood: '*Amerikai*?'

Guessing that the mob had taken us to be Americans

I replied, with a roar of laughter: '*Amerikai*! *Na khoob*!' This threw the heavies. I immediately pulled out the sign I had painted on a section of sheet to explain that we were friends. It said: "English" in Persian script. This confused them at first until some smart fellow pointed to the fact that the sign was upside down. '*Englisi*?' they cried. I laughed hilariously again. '*Englisi, khoob; Amerikai, na khoob*!' The mob was not amused. It seemed that the Americans and the English were just as bad.

Fortunately, with the gathering getting ugly, a charming Iranian policeman came to my rescue, and the crowd dispersed. This comic, almost tragic, confrontation had its roots in events nine years before in 1953: the ousting of Mohammad Mossadegh, the incredibly popular elected Prime Minister who had nationalised the British oil interests in Iran. A subsequent coup by the CIA and the British led to the restoration of the Shah, who had fled the country. I am indebted to Stephen Kinzer's book *All the Shah's Men* for his description of this international debacle.

Mohammad Mossadegh was born in 1881 into one of the rich land-owning Persian families. He was educated in France and Switzerland. The struggle over Persia at that time was between Britain and Czarist Russia with the young Mossadegh opting for the former. He was elected to parliament in 1915 and in due course he became governor of the province of Fars, later of Azerbaijan. His great strength lay in his ability to mesmerize crowds by his speechmaking.

His Imperial Majesty Mohammed Reza Shah Pahlavi, Shahanshah of Iran in September 1941, at the age of 21 years and 11 months, succeeded his father Reza Khan who, as Commander-in-Chief of the Army, had been elected Shah in December 1925.

Princess Ashraf, the dynamic and forceful twin sister of the Shah was born in 1920. Ashraf said about herself: 'I was volatile, quick tempered rebellious (and small)'. She shared her father's qualities of stubbornness, fierce pride and iron will. 'I have always tried to love anyone who is an important part of my brother's life,' she claimed. The CIA thought she was forceful and scheming and eager to co-operate to bring about the fall of Mossadegh.

In 1950, Mossadegh visited Princess Ashraf and they argued over his relationship with her father, the previous Shah – they were now enemies.

He told her about the Oil Commission which he chaired. 'The funding of so much in the future will depend on our getting control of our oil assets, rather than let Britain take nearly all the revenue.'

She, however, wanted to discuss the Imperial Organization for Social Services, which she had just set up. 'In the rural villages it was not unusual for a whole family to live on the yield of a date palm and a pair of scrawny goats. Living on the barest subsistence level, these people had no buffers at all against any form of natural catastrophe, such as epidemic, earthquake, or drought.'

He agreed: 'Little has changed since I was Governor of Fars province thirty years ago. We need the oil money to build the roads to these remote villages, so we can take out the food and medical supplies.'

She asked him if he could suggest more directors for her organisation. He replied: 'Of course most of my friends left politics during your father's dictatorship. And then he sent me to prison. I was arrested for no reason at all, and imprisoned in Birjand, on the edge of the great Khurasan desert. I tried to commit suicide rather than be murdered in jail as others were. Only when my son approached your brother pleading for clemency, was I released. Your brother was very brave to ask your father on my behalf.'

She accused him of always being against her father, which he denied: 'When he was the Minister of War, he asked me to be Minister of Finance. He wanted to reform and expand the Ministry of War. He suggested I could bring order to the country's public finance. I remember he said I could use my theoretical and practical knowledge to the benefit of the country. I agreed to become the Minister. Later he asked me to be Governor of Azerbaijan and I agreed. No, I admired your father's energy. But in October 1925, I opposed the Bill that made him a dictator.'

She said he opposed the Trans Iranian Railway that her father had built.

'To transport arms to Russia in the war', he replied.

'Stalin was grateful when I met him.'

'And he gave you a priceless sable coat. And he expected us to ratify a Soviet-Iranian Oil Agreement.'

In April 1951, Princess Ashraf met her brother after the Parliament had voted 79-12 that Mossadegh should be Prime Minister after it had agreed his condition that it would approve his Oil Nationalisation Bill. She threatened the Shah that she would leave Iran if he did not get rid of Mossadegh. He replied that he must stick by the Constitution and let Mossadegh become Prime Minister.

In October 1951, Dean Acheson, US Secretary of State to President Harry Truman, welcomed Mossadegh to Washington and congratulated him on being chosen by *Time* magazine as its Man of the Year for 1951. Acheson suggested that some in the CIA thought that Mossadegh supported the Soviets, which he denied: 'My record is clear. I am a convinced democrat. I allow the Tudeh Communist Party to function freely but I never embrace their policies. In fact I abhor the Communist doctrine and have rigorously excluded Communists from my government. The Tudeh Party may be well organized but it is not powerful. Secretary, you must understand that my sole wish is to solve the oil question.' Acheson offered to help with the British.

In January 1953, with Eisenhower now elected as President, General 'Beedle' Smith, Director of the CIA, met

Kim Roosevelt, who was the grandson of Theodore Roosevelt and head of the Middle East Department of the CIA. His effectiveness as an agent and organizer was attested to by Kim Philby, the British diplomat turned Russian spy, who called him 'the quiet American ... the last person you would expect to be up to his neck in dirty tricks.' He was charming and shrewd. Beedle said: 'It's over a year since Mossadegh went home after he charmed the United Nations. The new British Conservative Government didn't accept Acheson's formula for a solution. It insisted that Mossadegh "had to fail, to be crushed and punished". So he kicked out the Brits and he is still in power.' They planned the coup.

On 16th July in a hotel on the French Riviera, Princess Ashraf met the Senior British SIS Operative, who explained the dangerous mission she was being asked to undertake, to return to Tehran and persuade her brother to back the coup. She accepted a donation towards her gambling debts and a white fur coat.

In 11 days in August 1953 the coup went from failure at the first attempt to its final success:

- Ashraf failed to persuade the Shah to support the coup.
- Roosevelt threatened the Shah that he would leave Iran if the Shah didn't go along with the coup and sign the royal decrees sacking Mossadegh.
- Roosevelt and his team celebrated the forthcoming coup.
- The royal decrees didn't get to Shah before he flew off to his summerhouse near the Caspian Sea.
- The decrees arrived back by road.
- The first attempt at the coup failed as Mossadegh had found out about it.
- The royal decrees were then stenciled for distribution,

the communists demonstrated against the Americans and the shah, who then left the country for Iraq and then Rome.
- 'Beedle' Smith told Roosevelt to come home, but he refused. Instead he told the US Ambassador to visit Mossadegh.
- The Ambassador blamed Mossadegh for anti-American protests and denied any involvement in a coup. Mossadegh then appointed a Royalist as the new Tehran Police Chief, who released the plotters.

On the morning of 19th August, after the CIA had passed on copies of the decrees to the newspapers, they published fake interviews with the Shah's appointed replacement for Mossadegh. Pro-Mossadegh papers and those supporting the communists were ransacked or set on fire. The government radio station was taken over. Pro-Shah troops took control of the main squares.

The main turning point was when the mob from the bazaar, led by the Zirkaneh giants, the enormous weightlifters, wielding their huge barbells followed by CIA paid thugs, such as 'Brainless' Shaban and 'Icy' Ramazan, plus a column of prostitutes including 'Sugar-lip' Zeynab and 'Saucer-eyed' Azam, marched towards the city centre. CIA-supplied money was handed out to those that joined the parade. Mossadegh escaped from his home and was arrested next day.

In September a military court sentenced Mossadegh to three years' solitary confinement in prison. In a moving speech he said: 'My only crime is that I nationalized the Iranian oil industry, and removed the network of colonialism, and the political and economic influence of the greatest empire on earth from this land ... My life, reputation, person and property – and those of others like me – do not have the slightest value compared with the lives, the independence, the greatness and the pride of millions of Iranians, and the

IRAN TO TEHRAN AFTER THE CIA COUP

future generations of this people.' He died on March 5th 1967 aged 85.

On 4th September, Roosevelt returned to Washington where he was welcomed as a hero and offered the job of running a coup in Guatemala against Colonel Arbenz who had been elected a couple of years before.

Only later can we look back and see that the CIA coup in Iran was a turning point in the history of the Middle East and the start of the American Empire.

Next year in Guatemala, Arbenz was ousted and a brutal military dictatorship took over. This led to a vicious civil war from 1960 to 1996, with democracy restored in 1986.

In 1956, the Americans cancelled the elections in Vietnam as Ho Chi Minh would have won them. As a young man in 1919 he had petitioned the Paris Peace Conference demanding Vietnamese independence. Nineteen years after cancelling the elections, the US left Vietnam after bombing neighbouring Laos and invading Cambodia in 1970. This led to the brutal Khmer Rouge regime.

In 1961 the CIA carried out the fiasco of the Bay of Pigs invasion of Cuba.

They were already involved in the assassination of the Congo's democratically elected Patrice Lumumba and replacement by Joseph Mobutu, one of the world's most brutal and corrupt dictators.

Three years later, the CIA replaced President Goulart of Brazil by a repressive military regime, which remained until 1985.

In the same year they defeated Peru's civilian government's attempt to control their biggest oil company, Standard Oil of New Jersey.

In the following year in the Dominican Republic, the US crushed a popular uprising, which wanted to return to power Juan Bosch who had been elected in 1962 but was then ousted by a military regime.

In 1967 Sukarno, who got rid of the Dutch colonizers in Indonesia, was forced out and replaced by General Suharto, who instigated what the CIA acknowledged, in terms of numbers killed, was one of the worst mass murders of the 20th century.

In 1973, the elected president in Chile, Salvador Allende, was ousted by a CIA coup and replaced by General Pinochet who then murdered more than 3,200 of his opponents.

Much of this period in American history can be blamed on the paranoia generated by the Cold War. Sadly since its ending in 1990, US hegemony has continued.

CHAPTER 8
SOUTH IRAN OR AFGHANISTAN?

Sunday 22nd July

Meanwhile I had found garage and we eventually got lift from there in sort of lorry-cum-bus going to Qom.

One of those sitting in front spoke very good English and through him we didn't have to pay. However it proved a long (time) ride for 80 miles. The passengers were all going to the Holy City of Qom for a religious festival and spent much time singing chants, which required responses – quite serious. They were not terribly keen on us singing.

Our first stop was at a delightful tea-house with a large pond in the middle surrounded by trees and tables and also that characteristic of Iranian tea houses – the low Persian carpet covered table for sitting on. We talked with Persian who didn't like his food, earned about £12 a week for good job, said how difficult it was to get passport – almost impossible for student who hadn't done *service militaire*.

We drove on and stopped in middle of desert to sleep as pilgrims didn't want to arrive till morning. Sleeping on the stony sand is not comfortable!

John's card from Tehran, Sunday morning, 22nd July

Only the one letter from you. Hence very miserable. <u>Please</u> write to Lahire, Pakistan. Getting news from home cheers one up a great deal. 24 hours wait at border with flies and mosquitos wasn't much fun. But luck changed when 2 Pakistanis took us to Tehran. Whether they take us on or not is doubtful but I hope to goodness they do as things are very hot and fly ridden. Persians nothing like as nice a people as Turks but it is too soon to form an opinion. A postcard will come when I get to India but these are so much quicker. If you would like me to phone you on your birthday at 9 a.m. your time please let me know in all your letters in case I miss any. August 10th I think!! Very much looking forward to October – hope you are. I'll write again in a few days. See you soon (2 months). All my love John.

Monday 23rd July

Woke 5.30 and got back on road. We hitched from first tea-house stop and got private car into Qom. Religious festival was beginning and chanting columns of black-shirted men strode down the street, many carrying banners.

On edge of Qom started hitching and got another private car to where by-pass joined. Met some topologists taking readings by side of refreshing stream.

After short wait got lift on coke truck. No room in cab so we both sat on a couple of sacks on top of the coal – very hot travelling through the semi-desert and not terribly comfortable. After a while I went inside and co-driver went up on top with John and made obscene suggestions while the driver and I sang to each other in the cab.

We stopped for lunch and had pretty foul meal consisting of aubergines and fatty meat – possibly coming from the horse. We hitched, wrote and slept until they were ready to go and for the most of the rest of the trip I was on top alone while John was in the cabin with the other two. Up top it was very good but a little windy. I couldn't turn my back because of coal dust blowing back. Interesting to see how

SOUTH IRAN OR AFGHANISTAN?

one's mind is taken off discomfort by poetry or some other distraction.

Arrive Isfahan quite late and had time for quick meal before it got dark: kebab cooked on open-air charcoal fire, tomatoes, bread and melon for 1/9 each!

Long taxi ride out of Isfahan which we both regretted not seeing. Soon it became apparent there was no traffic and as we had no less than three offers from people to stay the night with them we accepted the first which fortunately was right on the road to Kerman.

We were led by our bespectacled large-nosed Persian host into his house and were impressed by its beauty – the front door brought us into a large courtyard in the middle of which was a pool and into which was pumped the water for washing. We washed and went to the toilet – an incredibly primitive affair for such a house – no paper, no flushing and no seat.

We were then led up some steps at the far end of the courtyard and were taken through a porch dividing the two main parts of the house onto a balcony overlooking the garden. The garden was more of an orchard and did not seem to have any flowers or grass and consisted of just rows of trees separated by irrigation channels and the odd path. Our room seemed to be the balcony, which was covered with a magnificent Persian carpet as indeed so it seemed were all the rooms in the house. As far as one could make out there were no chairs, perhaps nothing raised at all. We sat on the hard uneven stone of the balcony made tolerable by the carpet but really very uncomfortable.

Our host could speak very little English and really relied on one or two phrases for conversation: 'I only little English speak' and 'My mother is very glad, my sister is very glad, my brother's father is very glad'. The piece occurred frequently, usually with some additional member of the family tagged on the end. Any explanation at relationships was disastrous. He had his uncle in the house and referred to him always as my 'brother's father'.

He seemed a very young 24. We were offered a cup of tea, which was made by a brother who took an unbelievably long time to prepare the great brew. It was very good but our host insisted on putting in about as much sugar as tea! The tea was made with a wonderful urn heated by a charcoal fire and the teapots were kept hot on another charcoal fire. We had the brass spoons that we had only seen once before at the peasant village in Turkey.

While we talked various delightful little children scampered round the house stopping every now and then to gaze shyly but inquisitively at the foreigners. Although we saw the mother and sister walking round there was obviously no question of them coming to join us. They were not veiled but not much more than their eyes was left uncovered by the great robe, which formed their only clothing. Even the uncle got no further than shaking hands.

The appearance of the wireless prompted an exhibition of the Twist from John and myself. We weren't sure it went down well! Like all Iranians this one seemed unable to tune his wireless.

We eventually accepted the offer of food – anything to relieve the discomfort of the floor; but had to wait for the other brother who spoke slightly better and less apologetic English. Our host did not stop apologizing from the moment we saw him until we left. He even greeted us in the morning with 'I am very sorry'.

We ate at about 11 (at which time the youngest in the family were going to bed!) on the balcony floor off a large platter on which was kebabs, bread, yoghurt, some mint-like leaf and cucumber. There are no knives and forks – all with hands. We eventually said goodnight and settled down to a fairly hard and short night.

SOUTH IRAN OR AFGHANISTAN?

Tuesday 24th July

I was woken by the cat practically putting claws in my face and the harsh and piercing caws of the crows in the high trees above.

We started to hitch about 5.30 and found things going badly – got first lift to Benzine station just out of town. The lift was one of the fastest we had on a lorry. The petrol station was very large with a pool in the middle relieved by a fountain. The actual garage was more like a mosque than a garage with beautiful tiling. An effort had been made to grow grass at either side and the whole effect was very good. We were promised all sorts of lifts and told all sorts of times when various means of transport would leave – all fictitious.

John went back into Isfahan to get money and post. Many people spoke English and were very helpful. The Post Restante had only about 20 letters and 5 were for us! Meanwhile I was left to ward off the sun by myself.

We got a lift to Nain in a lorry that seemed doomed from the very start. We had various stops and the people were very kind. They bought us dinner – horrible kebab and bean salad – ugh! The rattling over the roads came to an end at some remote village in the middle of the desert. It was big trouble and the back wheels had to come off – back axle etc. There was an old blind man in the truck with us who for all his infirmity was very agile. The kind young man who spoke English had his wife with him and three children. The wife was very beautiful. She did not eat with us or make any attempt at communication at all.

The repair took so long that we saw the sun go down in the desert. It is wonderful the way the heat of the day can give to such a cool and beautiful evening – with only the wind to break the perfect silence. There was a shallow lake at the back and John had a swim.

We left and by now sleep was the only thing to do in the

lorry. Unfortunately the blind man was taking up rather a lot of room.

We rattled our way through the cool of the evening and eventually reached Nain about 11 p.m. There we decided to have some restless hitch-type sleep in front of what looked very like a railway waiting room but was in fact a roadhouse conveniently situated next to the benzine station.

Our evening was enlivened by the presence of a really remarkable old man dressed in long black cloak and green turban. The most striking thing about him was the way he smoked his long leather bound pipe. Every now and then he would inhale with tremendous ferocity – the result being that he would emit smoke for the next minute or so. He also carried a tin sandwich box with him full of sweets tasting rather like icing sugar. He offered these to everyone – including ourselves – within range. Most remarkable of all he did everything with a very abrupt movement very rapidly acting on some inward impulse.

We slept, me on a wooden bench outside the teahouse, John on the stone pebbles surrounding the garage. Whilst I slept John hitched on and off the whole night, often getting up with sleeping bag on him!! The people in the teahouse were very worried that our kit would get taken but assured and amused then by mime of speedy awakening and quick knife drill on would be assailant.

John's card from Yazd, Iran, Wednesday 25th July

Camels – sifting sand – men with slings like David. This is really the new world for us. We eat with our hands out of the communal pot and tea is drunk from the saucer. The dead part of Iran is to come. Yesterday we waited 8 hours without luck in hot sun. Then truck comes along which collapsed in the desert. 3 hours later the wheels have been removed and put back. We

SOUTH IRAN OR AFGHANISTAN?

went on through the desert. Dust is everywhere and we ain't half dirty. This is Wednesday in Yazd, south central Iran – try and find on a map. It's a really big shanty town. All my love John.

Wednesday 25th July

We got a lift at about 6.00 on a bus to Yazd. We had to seduce the driver to get him to take us at all but much *Pool nadoram* – 'I have no money' – and big grinning got us inside. We were put on two wooden stools in the gangway and suffered (I at any rate as John was soon offered a proper seat) agony for as long as we were raced – at least 50 mph – over the rough corrugated desert road. My insides were given such a terrible shaking so much so that I suffered a temporary ruptured muscle in my right side.

First thing in Yazd, we parked in front of bicycle shop and I went to post some letters. I was soon picked up by an Iranian who spoke English. The post office was the usual many-roomed tumble down affair and they didn't really understand the meaning of airmail. However they eventually worked out the price – 11 toman for each (1/1d). This was obviously a mammoth sum and so they suggested we put three cards in one envelope and send them off! In fact I had to settle for 4 large stamps per card, which they insisted on putting on. Next need was toilet – very difficult word to communicate.

Meanwhile John had left the kit in the hospitable care of the cycle shopkeeper and gone to buy bog roll. He was taken half-a-mile down the road to a shop where there wasn't any and was redirected back to a shop next to the bicycle shop! Typical example of Iranian directions – helpful but mis-guided. The roll cost 3/-. By this time we had bought some bread and sat down in front of the shop to eat the very solid round bread, lemon and sugar surrounded by a crowd of children.

After this we took a taxi out to the petrol station on the Kerman road. We were followed out by the student and then waited until about 11 a.m. when the bus came along for Kerman. They wanted to charge some astronomical price but our friend told the driver we had no money and we got the 250-mile ride for 5/- each, which if we had travelled 6,000 miles the same way would have worked out at £7 each! We sat huddled up on the back seat but although not very comfortable had been honoured above people who had got on the bus with us, who had paid the full fare and were sitting in the gangway. The man in front with rather a square Teutonic face and crew cut took a dislike to John when he put the hat on his side and in common with quite a few other people on the bus was very interested to find out how much we paid. There was a very poor family sitting on the back seat with us including a mother and child who breast-fed her young from time to time.

We made many stops during the day and at one point came across our first view of a famous fire-worshipping sect inhabiting certain villages in the area. They were remarkable most of all for their black bowler hat like trilbies, which without exception they wore. They also had very long shirts and were mostly tall. At another place we were pestered by an old man singing – although it was a religious chant it seemed to cause the other bus travellers as much amusement and annoyance as it caused us.

We arrived about 12.00 at Kerman and walked over to the roundabout where the road led off to Bam and Zahedan. We slept on a raised part of the pavement practically under a street light but unmolested.

Thursday 26th July

Up at about 4.30, beginning to feel very tired. As usual there seemed to be nothing doing. Very early on we were

SOUTH IRAN OR AFGHANISTAN?

offered a lift for about 60 miles – free. Later on in the day we would have given our eyes for it. As it was we got nothing but 'money', 'money' all day. Because of the intensely mercenary attitude we perhaps sensed a hostility that wasn't there. We should rather have been thinking how wonderful it was that people should ever take us for free at all.

John had a recurrence of Gypo so we bought some rice (3/- very expensive) and boiled it on the square. Interesting to find out that oranges and lemons are only available in winter. We saw further examples of uninhibited physical contact between the men.

We were both very irritable but our tempers were completely abated by the discovery of a school where there was a large pool and I washed there and John went afterwards and had a swim before being chased out by the old guardian. As usual we were given a whole heap of information concerning buses, lorries etc., which were leaving at specific times but which of course didn't. Much of the day lorries passed and we hitched the same ones many times – much to their annoyance. There was for much of the day a lorry, which went round the square sprinkling water on the dust but it seemed to blow away just the same. I would have thought that especially with the locals the old adage 'If you can't fight them, join them' would be most applicable. It certainly works with flies. There was also a man who spent a good deal of the day watering the patch of grass in the middle of the roundabout.

The first sign that we were to get a lift came when a golden-toothed, tall, swarthy man drove round the square in a 12-seater bus-like machine. After much bargaining we got the price down to 5/- from 15/-. We made for the two remaining seats in the back but were soon assured that these were not for us – instead we were bundled into the back like luggage and watched while the bus slowly began to fill.

It was fascinating to watch the bartering that went on for

places and how one man refused a certain uncomfortable seat for a certain sum of money; however he came back later. There was much counting of money and much sharing out and eventually even the driver's percentage came under discussion and argument.

For the first part of the journey there were 26 people in the bus – 6 of them sitting in the luggage. I was in a quite impossible position – the man next to me seemed to be sitting on the point of John's rucksack. The kid sitting next to John had a painful cut on his foot – he was in the corner, terribly squashed, very big brown eyes, big head, sad eyes and thin body. At the first stop everyone got out and we were relieved. We bandaged man's sceptic finger from our medical kit and gratitude was expressed in grapes and sweets.

John rushed off because he thought the bus was leaving! We had to take luggage out and it occurred that bus might not be taking us. John had altercation with driver who took his hat and then tried to take his matches. Then big bales were put in back.

Our companions this time were an old peasant and his very beautiful gypsy type (with brown eyes and long hair) wife or daughter with her baby. The runt of odd-job boy, animal like and entirely dirty and obnoxious, knew only one English word: 'Fuck'. He tried to get in after us but we wouldn't let him so he had to hang on the outside. There was a man in the bus who said he was a Scot but couldn't speak a word of English.

The little kid showed John his foot and pleaded so John promised to bandage it up. He also had large spot marks on his arm – possibly after effects of malaria. There was a fight for the window. The little kid thought John wanted the window opened and so fought with man in front who wanted his part of the sliding panel opened.

At the second stop I got out and heard a strange noise behind me; the old man stumbled out being violently sick.

SOUTH IRAN OR AFGHANISTAN?

We went into roadhouse to eat. We saw many people eating eggs and relented on our decision not to spend any money. We eventually had 4 each. We were not so popular here because we found ourselves sitting at table with all in European clothes while others sat on carpeted stone slab and ate out of communal bowl. Kitchen very weird – red glow and white clad figure stoking.

Scot had little boy as brother. Scot terribly pockmarked. Man in front with plenty of room while others squashed. We went out and I walked straight into the stream! When we got in the menace joined us. Every time we started the religious chant came out, sometimes instigated by the runt. At next stop bicycle got down from on top and they threw my rucksack to the ground. Next stop the musician who had played on his primitive, weird, biblical, flute-like instrument broke John's rucksack strap and laughed so left – really primitive.

The last part of trip everyone terribly tired. Fell asleep in any position, hands and feet going anywhere. The runt had come from his animal-like clinging on the outside and joined us. We arrived in Bam about midnight and walked to the Benzine station and slept under the austere eye of two locked petrol pumps. We were both exhausted and I certainly never slept so well.

Friday 27th July

We woke about 4.30 and there was a lorry down the road waiting to go to Zahedan. The driver was asleep so John had the brilliant idea of making him a cup of tea for when he awoke. Things seemed to be going pretty well and the driver accepted the tea although not with the gratitude we might have expected from him. It soon became apparent that he wasn't going to play ball so we had to try someone else.

While cooking tea a great crowd of children had come up

and when the primus packed up there was as usual some local who knew how to get it performing properly even though it was at the expense of singeing his hair. I had tried someone else for a lift and it seemed that everyone on the truck except the driver wanted us – *tant pis*!

The children were very pleasant but out for anything they could get. They finally had to settle for addresses, which they devoured eagerly until our patience was exhausted. They wanted everything we could give them.

It was not long before an old man came up, took me by the arm and led me over to a turbaned lorry driver – a very large thick set man who looked like the Pakistani we later found out he was. The old man told me to show all my money (we had decided on 15/-) and I collected it from John, who gave it to the Pakistani and we eagerly awaited the outcome of what looked like a promising lift. After a while the driver got into his cab and started up the road. John jumped on the running board just in case!

We loaded our kit into the back of the empty truck. Inside it was very deep and we were to be grateful for the cover it afforded us against the sand and heat. We went for a few hundred yards then stopped while the crew had a rest. Our companions for the first part of the trip were a couple of heavy bales and a stoop of chicken. The dust in the air was so thick that the sun was just a white ball of light without glare. We sat for most of the daylong ride with wet towels over our heads. Even though water was very warm, evaporation made it cold. We were somehow protected in the lorry but every time we stood up to peer over the top the heat hit us like a furnace.

After the next stop a man got in with his child and finding no other place set down on top of the two bales, which we had thought so precious. He did not seem at all happy largely because of the discomfort to his sweet little child. He was at great pains to give him a drink of our very warm water and

SOUTH IRAN OR AFGHANISTAN?

tried to get him to drink out of our large flask but this only served to jar his teeth out of position. We then succeeded with a mug at the same time as amusing the son with our clucking noises. Although the father's smile took more drawing out.

The desert was the real thing, nothing but a sea of soft sand stretching as far as the dust would allow us to see. At about 12.00 we arrived at a real oasis, palm trees, the lot. The freshness inside the mud-walled hut was wonderful after the desert heat. This was perhaps due to the presence of an enormous refrigerator.

Having supposedly given our last money to the Pakistani, who was very charming, we were unable to buy anything to eat and had to rely on his hospitality. For lunch he offered us large quantities of melon then he ate a kebab and we all went to sleep on the hard wickerwork covered slabs for 3 hours during the heat of the day.

At about 4.00 we started off again, still at the same fast pace (the lorry was empty) as before although there were places where the road seemed to disappear altogether and all the driver could do was follow the telegraph poles. We were joined at one stage by a turbaned local, who distinguished himself by climbing out of the lorry by stretching his leg right up to the sky, grasping the wire across the top of the lorry with his foot and climbing out. We travelled on into the night and although the heat abated the dust didn't. Eventually we stopped right up in the mountains and when we shone our torch the powerful beam showed only clusters of rock formations as though we were in some enormous cavern. We sat down on the stony sand and the Pakistani brought out a bundle wrapped in a handkerchief. He opened it up and we saw to our surprise a chicken and some bread and an enormous beaker of yoghurt. Thus we settled down to eat in the silence of the heights under the stars. A woman with us in the desert ate by herself.

On arrival in Zahedan, we were so exhausted that we slept on the pavement where we were dropped at 1.00 in the morning.

Saturday 28th July

Slept night on until 6.00 in spite of passers-by. We started to try and make some tea and the primus wouldn't work. Meanwhile I went off to try and buy some fat to cook eggs. We were again given breakfast by the occupants of the house in front of which we were camped. They even supplied a blanket to sit on. We had numerous cups of tea.

Then Roberto, the local wide-boy, came along and introduced himself as the Tourist Guide. He was no more than a money-changing spiv. He had long greasy hair, an arse that stuck out, a swagger and an air of conceit that one would have thought would have repulsed all the locals. His great remark: 'If there is anything I can do to help' meaning 'I wonder if we can help me'.

Anyway he took us to a form of hotel and we sat down on a couple of beds and discussed money and goods to be sold. We sold him our Thermos Flask for 10/- and it only cost 13/6! Good business! We also bought £5 worth of Pakistani Rupees from him. When he realised we weren't going to sleep in the room, he became less friendly. When he came back having changed the money and I looked to see what the picture was on the note he seemed positively offended and went away leaving us to pay for the tea, which we had presumed he was offering us. However we did have a free and very thorough wash.

'Bob' then left us and all his promises of buses, cars etc. to Quetta vanished into thin air as we stepped out into the unfamiliar streets of Zahedan. Fortunately we soon found some friends and they showed us a hotel for 2/- a night which seemed worth one try at any rate. A most unprepossessing entrance led into a small courtyard in the middle of which was a pool where all the washing was done. Having settled into the room, which had nothing but two wooden beds with a blanket thrown over them we were led to the swimming pool by our two friends who did everything for us and spent much of the time showing us the post office, hotel and swimming pool. We got back after the swim, which was not as great as might have been largely because of the very cold wind and largely because of our extreme exhaustion accentuated by having had to cycle with the local population up to the pool. We cycled – they sat on the back. When we returned to the hotel for a siesta, two soldiers were making use of bunks, one with the smelliest socks ever. They were much worse two days later! We had a siesta then made a great meal of onion soup and eggs, which was much admired by the local population, especially the manager who was tall, had dark crew-cut hair and the inevitable squint. He came to see us many times during our stay, together with the rest of the 'staff'. Went to bed very early.

John's card from Zahedan, Iran

The toughest part is now over. Late last night we arrived here in Zahedan after a long day's ride through a sandstorm in the back of a lorry. The desert was the bleakest I have ever seen and the sight of an oasis where we drank warm salty water was the only hope in the wicked country. From now on to Quetta in Pakistan we take a train as there is only the railway. There are no roads over the desert – one has to follow the telegraph poles. Thank goodness India is so near for we are terribly dirty and this country is very dusty. I will write again soon but from now on we are in a civilised world. I hope the Skaw is hot now and you are doing plenty of sailing. All my love John.

Sunday 29th July

Got up quite late, met Pakistanis who had got into money difficulties and wanted our Sterling. They were charming – living in a sort of compound for Pakistanis, many of whom were permanent residents and were begging to buy anything they could from Pakistanis who had just arrived.

The hotel started to fill up during the day; the most interesting arrival being an American who had travelled extensively in South-East Asia and was in many ways pro-Communist. He talked a lot about Vietnam and how the Vietcong were the people to side with. He said there were many pro-Communists in S.E. Asia. People are fed which they are not in India. Hong Kong and Rio are great places to see.

He told us a horrific story about an American family travelling through Iraq. Their car breaks down and they are invited into a nearby house. The wife is raped and the husband is murdered. Then the wife is murdered. The child has been allowed to watch it all and is then killed. The men who raped the wife start fighting and then the police come.

John's thoughts on Southern Iran

Hitchhiking becomes an obsession. It is the opposite of tourism. The aim is to reach a destination in the minimum time possible. Ostend to Amritsar in India measures 9,000 km. To hitch this in 22 days before motorways for nearly all the way is sheer lunacy. Yet this is what Andrew and I achieved, if one strips out days of illness and rest.

There is an Iranian proverb, which says, 'Isfahan is half the world'. It is probably the most beautiful city in Iran. Our final lift dropped us out of town for our next leg of our journey. Andrew guarded the rucksacks whilst I hitched

SOUTH IRAN OR AFGHANISTAN?

into the centre of the city to pick up a letter at the Central Post Office from Jannie. There wasn't one. A tourist would have walked the ten minutes from there to the Naqsh-e Jahan Square, the second largest square in the world. Surrounded by exquisite mosques it would have offered me a life-long memory. But I was in a hurry and returned immediately to carry on hitchhiking. One day I hope I can go back, this time with Jannie.

Iran is a great plateau of desert and barren mountains. Oases offered the traveller a break, a jug of cold water and a watermelon, cool from being stored in windowless mud houses. After the incident in Tehran, there was sometimes a tension in the air, perhaps because we attempted to get lifts for free whilst in Iran the locals were expected to pay. Or perhaps this slight antagonism was a residual of years of British involvement in the country.

In general we were met with friendship. This went a stage too far as we crawled across the desert in a coal truck. Andrew, as usual, entertained the driver in the cab. I sat on the pile of coal contemplating the view. Suddenly, from the cab appeared the face of the co-driver. With a huge grin he climbed up to sit next to me. He had a cunning plan, which I had to refuse; I explained that the night before I had enjoyed the company of ten buxom girls in Tehran and I was exhausted and not interested in his advance. This charade was acted out in fear of failure. He did not pursue his amorous advance. In case, the reader thinks this is an Iranian problem, I should mention a year before, whilst crossing the Mohave Desert in California, the amorous driver had managed to put his weapon through the passenger's window. Thank goodness for electric windows.

Arriving at Zahedan, the last town in Iran, we were faced with a dilemma. Do we continue hitchhiking into Pakistan and on to Quetta some 735km away, or cheat? In 1962 the train ran more frequently than the twice a month it is scheduled today. Nowadays the Baluchistan independence movement has a bad reputation for bombing the line. We cheated and entered this remote corner of the old British Empire by rail, the means of transport that held together the British Raj.

From the western corner where we entered the subcontinent it would take 4 days by train to the eastern corner beyond Dacca in today's Bangladesh. From Lahore, in the north it would take 2½ days to the southern tip of India. The Raj was immense.

Andrew would take 3 days on his return to London from Istanbul, a thrilling train trip in itself. But these great journeys are insignificant when compared to the trip across Russia from St. Petersburg to Vladivostok. It takes nearly seven days. The Soviet Empire was of a different scale.

In 1962, we skirted the Soviets, first in Germany and Austria, then in the Balkans and Turkey. Fear of the northern neighbour had permeated Turkish history, and made the West wary of Iran, in case the Soviets decided to seek a warm water port in the Persian Gulf. Even the case for our later war in Afghanistan was defensive against the perceived threat of Soviet access to the Indian Ocean in Baluchistan, particularly as a pipeline could be laid from the Central Asian oil fields.

In 1962, we were in a hurry and although tempted to hitch east from Tehran to Mashhad and through Afghanistan via Heart, Kandahar and Kabul and over the Hindu Kush to Lahore, which was less in distance, we realized it was probably longer in time than the southern route we chose. Within a few years the northern route was favoured by hippies with their long hair, unlike our short back and sides, and their taste for hashish smoked in the hookah pipes, which we were too innocent to appreciate, or heroin from the opium poppies that still flourish in Afghanistan. The hippie trail ended at the end of the 1970s with the Soviet invasion of Afghanistan and the Iranian revolution.

For a personal reason, I would have liked to have passed through Jalalabad, where, in January 1842, my ancestor Robert Waller was held hostage during the retreat from Kabul, which ended the First Afghan War, leaving 16,500 British Empire troops and followers dead, bar the solitary Doctor William Brydon. The National Army Museum's record for Lieutenant Waller is:

'Robert Waller (1808–1877) was gazetted as a second lieutenant with the Bengal Horse Artillery on 23 June 1827. Promoted to captain, he was sent to Kabul with the 1st Troop, 1st Brigade, Bengal Horse Artillery, in November 1840. He was taken hostage, with his wife Annie and their daughter Selina, on 9 January 1842, when Akbar Khan persuaded General Elphinstone to hand over several women, children and wounded officers in return for supplies and a safe escort for his army. The Wallers were released on 21 September 1842 after the British Army of Retribution reached Kabul. Waller later took part in both Sikh Wars and in operations on the North West Frontier in 1851–1852. He eventually retired with the rank of colonel in 1858.'

Here is a copy of the letter he sent home to his mother in Ireland whilst in captivity. It was printed in the Irish Times.

'The scenes we had to go through, as you may imagine, were frightful; such a retreat, in the depth of winter, without food, clothing or shelter – another whole country under snow!! The men's feet and hands were frozen off and they fell in the road by scores, while the enemy pressed on our rear with the impossibility of keeping them at a distance, our guns having been abandoned one after the other, the horses being incapable of drawing them and the hills on every side covered with the enemy's riflemen, who kept up a constant and destructive fire upon us, while at every check a general rush was made, attended by fearful slaughter, our men being almost incapable of making any resistance. A few days from the commencement of the retreat completed the destruction of the force – it was a dreadful time as we passed along over the dead and dying, the wounded and frost bitten of our comrades and friends. No questions were asked, no assistance to the wounded could be afforded, where they fell there they lay to be butchered in our sight by our enemy who spared none except a very few who happened to fall into the hands of the chief men – among who were myself, wife and child – I was severely wounded in the action previous to the retreat and have a bullet in my right side now which passed through my arm below the shoulder and before that I had been wounded in the head, but not severely. Akbar Khan has treated us with much more kindness and consideration than we had reason to expect under all circumstances. He supplied our wants to the best of his ability for we saved not an article or sixpence, having escaped but with the clothes on our backs, and for more than a fortnight we had nothing but these, day or night in the middle of winter, and having been on the bare ground or on the snow.

Negotiations for our release have been tried, but without success as yet. I believe, however, that Akbar is willing to make terms if they are not too hard upon him. He has promised to forward this letter for us, and I am going to send it open.'

In May 1842, Akbar Khan captured the Bala Hissar fortress in Kabul and became the new Emir of Afghanistan. He ruled for three years until his death. Some suggest he was poisoned by his father Dost Mohammed.

SOUTH IRAN OR AFGHANISTAN?

During the nineteenth century the rivalry between the British and Russian Empires led to conflict as these two giants competed for supremacy in Central Asia. Known as 'The Great Game', it is considered to have started in 1813 with the Russo-Persian Treaty after Russia's defeat of Persia and expansion south through khanates in the Caucasus to Azerbaijan. The Tsar then repeated the process in Central Asia, subduing the Khanates of Khiva, Bokhara and Khokand. The next stage on the route to India would have been the Emirate of Afghanistan. Lord Auckland, the Viceroy of India, assumed that Emir Dost Mohammed was sympathetic to the Russians so, in 1838, he launched the First Afghan War to replace him with the pro-British Shah Shuja. By 1841 the Afghans tribes, under the leadership of Dost Mohammed's son Akbar Khan, were ready to kick the British out of Kabul, which led to the tragic Retreat from Kabul.

Fast forward to 1979 when Ayatollah Khomenei threw out the Americans from Iran and the Soviets seized an opportunity to invade Afghanistan and install their own favourite. The Americans, Saudi Arabia and other Muslim countries funded the insurgency and now, over 200 years after it all started, this tragic land is still at war with itself.

Robert Waller's comment: 'Akbar Khan has treated us with much more kindness and consideration than we had reason to expect under all circumstances' perhaps sums up the honour of the Muslim host to treat his guest with hospitality.

The card I sent Jannie from Multan on our journey from Quetta to Lahore said it all: 'This is the most wonderful country I have ever been in'. The people were incredibly hospitable and of course spoke English. My friends in Gifto's Lahore Karahi Restaurant in Southall are the same. It is a tragedy that today the wars in Afghanistan spilling over into Pakistan would make such a journey, as we made in 1962, impossible.

CHAPTER 9
ANDREW COMPARES TURKEY AND IRAN

Istanbul – I was sitting in a mosque in Istanbul reading my tourist guide when a boy with a pigeon poking its head out from under his jacket came along and started yelling at me. I thought he was telling me that I couldn't read a tourist guide in a mosque. Anyway he soon left me in no doubt as to which way his feelings were directed for he spat powerfully and accurately at my toe through the iron gauze.

The further east we went, the more primitive people become. There seems an animal instinctiveness in the way people move and behave, especially the drivers and the pedestrians – collision is avoided with an uncanny certainty.

It seems that as the Indian concept of a beautiful woman is big-breasted, so is the Turks. Talking about film stars a man mentioned Diana Dors as being 'prima'!

A man said that of all European countries he liked Germany the best. This indicated to me that Turkey is moving towards America for Germany is the most Americanised of the European countries.

We had two dolmuş fares paid – one by charming Yugoslavian woman.

In Turkey, people have perhaps no conception of life without hardship. Houses of lowest class in Yugoslavia, Greece and Turkey are interesting pointers. In Yugoslavia, they are made of brick and cement but are poorly built with no colour. In Greece, they are of brick and cement, better built and with colour. In Turkey, they are made of mud and brick with no colour at all and often looking as though they

ANDREW COMPARES TURKEY AND IRAN

had been hollowed out of the ground and have earthy grassy roofs.

Street posters littered Istanbul. Men carried tremendous loads on their wood and leather carriers.

Eastern Anatolia – In the trip from Ağri to the last town before the frontier we were riding in the back of a Chevrolet truck. Sun was setting behind the great mountain ranges all around Mount Ararat on the right. There was the wonderful strength of nature and the insignificance of man. Riding away the West, life seems to become less important and less fearful. We saw the transience of animal life – a bird caught helplessly in telegraph wires. The glory of creation in the morning as the burning purity of the sun rises up swiftly from behind Ararat's neighbours. Ararat herself standing in solitary snow-covered magnificence seeming so close and yet rising 16,000 feet to the skies – its white top unaffected by the sun, which burns down on the village below.

The further east we go the less we see of the peasant woman, who remains in her home all day and only goes out for shopping. When she does, she is so heavily veiled that one can only see the eyes peeping out from two slits in the great loose gown she wears. This seems to be the source of the Latin conception of women for especially in poorer Italy and Spain they are very much the housewives and child-bearers.

Sex – In Istanbul, a Turkish friend told us about relations between men in Turkey. It is not unusual to hold hands etc. – they are completely uninhibited by physical contact.

Deformities – In Ankara, a boy who was part of the group around us, had no hands, just ill-formed stumps, an enormous head and squinting eyes. Later on in Turkey we saw a young man riding a tiny bicycle. His legs were minute and one was crossed beneath his stomach.

In Iran we saw a man walking on all fours as his legs were so short – he had shoes on his hands.

Dirt – Persia is by far the dirtiest country we have visited so far. Even in middle-class households, the lavatory is of the crouch, gymnastic, athletic type you'd never find in England.

The dust is terrible but that's nature's fault. It is the eating and drinking conditions that really revolt one. Water is always taken out of a communal beaker, which is never or rarely washed. The food is always kebab (lumps or minced on a skewer), which is eaten off great trays scorning the use of knives and forks. The trays never seem to be washed. The people themselves don't wash all that much either. Persia is the first country where, when you show somebody a bog roll, they don't know what it's for!

Eating – Although the food in Turkey was very greasy it did at least have variety. Kebab was only one of many dishes. In Persia, kebab is the only dish. It is eaten with a pancake-like bread, which is always tough unless absolutely fresh. In the teahouses it is not usually fresh. Also it is usually eaten with yogurt and onions.

In Turkey, there were salads. In Iran there are none. The food is often quite expensive, i.e. 3/- for a roadhouse kebab. However there is still the tea – not a luxury at 1d a glass. The Persians always drink their tea out of the saucer so it doesn't matter if the glasses aren't washed.

In Turkey we ate mousakas, pilau, veal and bread. Nothing seems to be drunk in Iran except tea and water.

Drinks – One of the things that put me off Persia at the start was the multitude of American bottled drinks that were being sold. These are not thirst quenching and seem, especially in such a hot country, to be a symbol of capitalism.

By contrast, the Turks, especially in Istanbul, drank their

own local made brews almost exclusively and they succeeded efficiently and pleasantly in slaking the thirst.

In Iran at first, we noticed one local drink – a highly liquid yoghurt usually served with a lot of salt and costing about 1d per glass.

There has been no sign of wine although the vintage we had in Istanbul was very similar to vinegar.

Animals – We have seen many different animals. The herons with their great wingspan, spindly legs and long red beak were first seen in Yugoslavia, where they existed in great profusion. They have appeared at frequent intervals since, even in the desert where their thinness seems to suit them to their arid surroundings.

At one of the last villages we went through before the Iran border we saw a heron's nest, which had been built on top of the v-shaped roof of a house. The nest was enormous, quite big enough for a man to get into.

Going through the desert, quite the most interesting animal was the camel – a great strong beast with its single hump, knobbly knees and laughing face. It moves its rider, who has to sway powerfully and rhythmically, with silent grace and majesty across the desert wastes.

Coming across one part of the Persian desert we saw someone hawking – the great bird tied with the customary leather thong to the wrist. Later we saw a huge white hawk ravenously attacking its kill – some creature looking very like a rabbit.

Of course, Iran is the country of the donkey. The poor creature had to be beaten constantly to make it move at all and others make a cry rather like a walrus. Its main features are its huge pair of ears and tremendous strength.

Children – Whereas in Turkey the children surrounded us every time we stopped at any village and were for the most part well behaved, in Iran we are very rarely surrounded by young children but always by 16+ year olds who practise their English on us unmercifully with always the same questions:

Where are you from?
Where are you going?
What is your name?
What is your work?
How many factories are there in America?

Art – The art, if anything, has been getting better. In Yugoslavia the paintings in the shops were terrible – really infantile. There were pictures of Tito in every shop.

In Turkey it was a little better. This time pictures of Atatürk were everywhere.

In Tabriz, we went round a number of art galleries. All the pictures were of a sickening lushness. The sensuality was quite unchecked. Most of the scenes portrayed seemed to be of Swiss-type landscapes – perhaps a sort of paradise to the Iranians. The colours too were completely unreal and very rich.

A corollary to the American drinks could perhaps be found in the conception of beauty. All the cards sold or pictures displayed were of big-breasted heavy-lipped women in decadent Hollywood style.

Music – In Turkey we had music everywhere – often Western classical mixed with Turkish folk music. From out of the primitive depths of Turkish wailing would emerge the ethereal strains of Bach's 'Jesu, Joy of Man's Desiring'.

The Turkish drivers enjoyed our singing very much and returned the compliment by giving many renderings of their own songs.

In Iran, the scene changed radically. There was hardly

any music at all, only religious chants requiring responses and the odd old man incanting some chants.

Religion – In Turkey, the Moslem religion didn't seem to have any hold on the people. Whereas in Persia it seems very strong.

Homosexuality – One would imagine from the way people behave in Turkey and Persia that there was a lot of homosexuality. It is, however, very different from the Western clandestine, corrupt homosexuality. Rather it is open and does not suggest the emotional ties, which are part of our conception of homosexuality.

CHAPTER 10
PAKISTAN AND PARTITION

Monday 30th July to Wednesday 1st August 5.00

Boarded train from Zahedan to Quetta in the evening and secured, thanks to dour German Siegfried, the last two top bunks. Thus we were three Europeans on top and 40 Baluchis underneath. They kept on piling in in spite of two empty carriages just down from ours. We decided not to pay to the border probably because of Siegfried's insistence that we shouldn't but then had to pay double the first part when buying tickets at the border. Train food was quite expensive but not bad. We managed to get 6 cups of tea for price of two.

John had an interesting conversation with man I first took to be the local doctor armed with microphone and length of rubber tubing. In fact it was an impressive ear trumpet. John's conversation went: 'Are you a Mohammedan?' 'No', 'Oh'.

Siegfried, who was also a scrounger, was the most unpleasant traveller we have come across: humourless, bursting with information and grumbling ceaselessly. No wonder he didn't enjoy his experience as much as us.

The two Pakistanis travelling with us were very charming and rather helped to introduce us to the caste system by their attitude to their countrymen.

There were some exciting incidents around the border as people tried to jump on and off, chased by bribe-hungry soldiers. The soldiers must do a good trade at their post – the last before the Pakistan border for to stay on the train the jumper has only to slip the soldier and he jumps off. (We saw this happen). We saw another who had jumped off being severely beaten by the train's policemen.

Andrew's first impressions of Pakistan

Class system at work as people in train opposite us on the platform would not allow other people obviously of inferior class get in. Two Pakistanis in our carriage talked of other Baluchis as animals yet would give money to a beggar.

On the station all the different class of waiting room, latrine etc. Where there had been bowls put in the toilets, people had come in and shat on the floor.

It seems to be the custom with all Pakistanis to pay for their guests. They even insist that is the way in Pakistan.

There seems to be a great contrast of peoples brought about by the class system.

They all wear pyjamas – enormous great loose trousers and long-tailed shirts, which are never tucked in and turbans used for everything.

Moslem religion is very strong with prayers 5 times a day.

The scavenging magpies get worse now we are in Pakistan. We saw some eating the eye off a dead cow. They are dirtier now than we have ever seen them.

Pakistani flies don't bother local population; they even crawl along people's teeth while they are asleep.

Music in Pakistan is often a cross between Scottish and Tyrolean.

Pakistani lorries – very colourful – all sorts of pictures painted on them. More often than not, the cabs look like nurseries.

The one track Pakistani roads make for very close passing and there are doubtless many accidents.

Life seems to be taken very easily with 4-hour break in middle of day and then continuous 20mph progress to destination 200 or 300 miles away.

Fortunately we have got off the hard Iranian slabs. These have been replaced by rope-sprung beds, which are vastly more comfortable.

Thursday 2nd August

Passed by Mukta in his Fiat about 150 miles from Quetta. During same ride they all got out to pray in the middle of the desert just after we had seen an enormous herd of camels – thousands strong. For the first part of ride passed through gorge by the side of the most beautiful river – a wonderful phosphorescent green. Saw men praying by the river miles from anywhere.

John met Pakistani at Quetta station who begged him to get him a visa. He wanted all information about the Pakistan Immigration facilities. Ride in jeep in morning to village where his seemed the only motor-powered vehicle. He bought us a pot of tea before leaving. In the evening arrived Jacobabad and were bought very good curry by the truck driver who had seemed too reserved for such generosity. We noticed how he gave money to a blind man, how the others didn't eat, at any rate, not with him. Saw first really undernourished child with horrible balloon shaped pot-belly.

At one stage in the ride we were joined by the first completely veiled woman we had seen – a sort of white headgear with gauze eyes.

Friday 3rd August

During stop for breakfast we saw terribly emaciated dog coughing pathetically in corner. Crossing magnificence of Lloyd Barrage over Indus. Saw man, shovelling shit off side of the road with his hands.

Police at Sukker took over hitching for us. He stopped a lorry and refused a bribe. Waiting outside Sukker having crossed the Indus. Given lift by truck which had been stopped by the police. They were not pleased but were delightful to us! Got lift about 10.30 then stopped. 3 hours for lunch and siesta during which time we had great wash down under pump and shirt washing supervised by another driver.

We found it impossible to pay for anything thus we couldn't without later embarrassment ask for anything. On the road we came across accident, surely one of many on these one-track roads where one gives way. We had puncture in afternoon caused by coming from soft sandy verge onto tarmac while passing a lorry. Used white roadside bricks to wedge lorry while repair done. Afterwards bricks thrown away not put back. Saw lorry that had back smashed in on level crossing – lorry worker (always rides on top) was killed.

Saturday 4th August

Things said about Multan:
  Graveyards, dust, beggars, heat are the four best things.
  In Multan you'll meet Lt. Edwards 1849 who conducted the siege of Multan.
  An old Persian proverb: Oh God, having made Multan, Sibi and Dadar, what need was there to make hell.
  Another Persian proverb: People found shivering in hell were from Multan.
  Waiting for a lift on outskirts of town, a missionary took us to his home and gave us breakfast of corn flakes, tea, toast, butter, marmalade and apple pickle!
  The rest of the journal for the day is based on our time with Robert Orr.
  On the subject of sex, we were taken down a street of brothels, which made Istanbul whores look like actresses
  There is complete segregation of sexes. Women all completely veiled except countrywomen who are semi-veiled.

Natural instincts suppressed in completely unnatural way – homosexuality, which we took for uninhibited relations between the men, is nothing more than lesser and stronger forms of perversion, which is rife throughout the East – D H Lawrence vindicated even out here. Young marriage is no solution – wives produce hordes of children and by 20 are old bags and husbands are fed up.

Multan has a population of 400,000 in an incredibly small area. Over-population is a great problem. Although there is enough food at moment, old bullock meat and poppadum form an adequate diet. There is a great disparity between rich and poor in Pakistan and there is no middle-class. There is communist infiltration although it will probably conquer India first. It is a solution to social injustice, which is so rife.

The hospital in Multan is supposedly the biggest in Asia – a White Elephant with inadequate staff. Even a drink of water has to be paid for. A woman died of a ruptured uterus without receiving transfusion, as there was no blood. Prisoners given 3 months relief for 1 pint yet say they would rather stay and leave prison a man!

Pakistan is 99% Muslim – a fanatical religion which the more educated see through. There is no great valuing of truth: Moses is Jesus' brother because (largely) Miriam was sister of Moses and Mary (synonym) mother of Jesus! Koran confuses this and thus God's word spread to Christians in one way and to Muslims in another.

The police are cowards and bullies, which does not surprise us although they are the hitchhiker's Godsend.

Much has been finely built but there is no maintenance – especially true of buildings although the roads and railways have been improved.

Muslim belief in fate helps alleviate the suffering caused by great poverty. Nelson probably said to Hardy 'Kismet' (it is fate) not 'Kiss me'.

Smallpox though not fatal leaves a terrible pockmarked

face and often causes blindness because of scales on the eyes. Cholera is non-existent here but dysentery is a greater disease. We must wash fruit in soap and water. The mangoes are the purest I've ever tasted.

Multan has 7 gates within old city wall and is over 2,000 years old. The streets are fantastically crowded with different areas for different products such as a street full of chemists. Posters are everywhere proclaiming in colour the owner of the shop and his wares. There are a fantastic variety of things sold. Green dye is used to colour hair red. They don't like white hair so some paint it black, which is not allowed – others paint it red. The shopkeepers are honest on the whole but always tell you the wrong price: for a gun, one shop asked 8 rupees, whilst another asked 4 rupees.

We visited tomb of some hero leader built 3 centuries ago. Inside in the middle was the tomb embellished by fake marble. Apparently everything like that is imitation although there were 3 pieces of beautiful green (red-veined) marble surrounding the bottom of the tomb. There were graves around the tomb, just white painted blocks of stone placed in rows like pews.

The people are very primitive. No cultural tradition at all which there was in Persia. Ornateness is one of the characteristics of building and art. Ostentation was a way of showing your money and position. This accounts for houses looking like stucco palaces with battlements and little towers.

In the tomb we had to take off our shoes and lay them on their sides so they would contaminate the ground as little as possible. We had to cover our knees too, being one of the sacred parts from umbilical to knees. This we did with borrowed tablecloths the locals wear.

The bazaar sold all sorts of nuts and grain etc. imaginable. Sugar, which was heavily rationed a few years ago, is now imported from Cuba following her loss of the American market. Rice should be long and mangoes firm. Potatoes are more expensive than onions and garlic was 8d for 2lbs!

A camel can walk for three days and nights without a stop at 5 m.p.h. It is much more valuable than a horse.

The Indus gets smaller towards the sea. The idea is to use the whole of the Indus-Ganges basin – great system of canals draining off water on all sides. Towns like Multan are entirely dependant on canals. Sometimes there is no rainfall, sometimes 10cms in 24 hours. Whole villages are washed away with their mud houses when covered by about 2ft of water.

First quality of Islam faith is hospitality – all are brothers. There is no caste system in Pakistan.

Missionary life is very hard – our host was suffering from ulcers. He had made 4 complete converts to Christianity. His wife was a doctor who ran missionary hospital.

Sanskrit is the basis for Urdu, Hindi, Hindustani and Farsi. Farsi is the polite language of Pakistan as French was for us the language of letters.

Flies and mosquitoes cannot breed in great heat or cold.

People told to get up and give us their seats in the bus. Then they could not sit down until 2 women, taking up double seats, moved together. 12 mile bus trip – 6p.

I was given rose in Multan to ward off every unfortunate eventuality.

John's card from Multan, West Pakistan, Saturday 5th August

Long time since I last wrote and we have gone across another frontier since then. Today is Saturday and we are at Multan, West Pakistan. We hitched through the night and even in this time things have changed. The camel is now equal to the ox and carries immense quantities. The tea has milk in and is very sweet – all boiled together and the weather is very hot. For two days now we pass through the desert either side of the Indus River. It is dry now but the rains are only 300 miles away. The Pakistan people have a code of hospitality, which must be seen to be believed. This is the most wonderful country I have ever been in. Dirt and hordes of people go together but as Muslims can eat meat this is much better than in India. Have received only letter but if all goes well will phone you August 10th 9.00 your time. All my love, John.

Sunday 5th August

Last ride in Pakistan – one of toughest and a great piece of hitching by John. The driver didn't give us time to get loaded and as truck moved off I was left hanging on outside with rucksack on my back. We then had to sleep on rock hard sacks of grain.

At one check point the controller was working out wages (or so it seemed) using English numerals. His maths was so bad that we supposed he was incompetent and cheating people in terms they didn't understand.

Monday 6th August

Arrived edge of Lahore at 3.00 in the morning, very tired. Went straight to sleep for 2 hours. Woken by flies as though every hair was being individually tickled.

Took bus for 6d to border and there searched at Indian customs. Took bus from border to Amritsar.

John's thoughts on the end of the Raj and Partition

From Multan, which is in the Punjab, we travelled the 230 miles to Lahore, the Pakistan Punjab capital and across where the Punjab state was divided in the tragic partition of India, just 15 years before our trip in August 1947, to Amritsar in India's Punjab state. We met people who regretted the awful events of the mass migration of 12 million people, when between ½ and 1 million died in the brutal circumstances of ethnic cleansing.

With the Second World War over in May 1945 and public opinion on the sub-continent strongly in favour of independence, the new Labour government in London realised it was time to bring to an end the Raj, or rule, that Britain maintained for nearly 200 years.

In 1929 it was decided to give different electorates to different religious communities so that they could be represented by their 'own' politicians. This hardened religious boundaries and led to the formation of the All India Muslim League, which wanted a separate Muslim homeland. During the Second World War the League expanded and claimed 2 million members.

The Indian National Congress, which was created in 1885, was, in the 1920s, under the leadership of Mahatma Gandhi. He demanded *swaraj*, literally meaning self-rule, to convey freedom from imperialism. By 1946 Congress had transformed itself into a mass party with 4.5 million members, and wanted a united, plural India, a home for all Indians.

The colonial state had been built on religious differences, with taps on railway platforms labelled 'Hindu water' or 'Muslim water'. In 1946, Gandhi lamented: 'A stranger travelling in Indian trains may well have a painful shock when he hears at railway stations for the first time in his life ridiculous sounds about water, tea and the like being either Hindu or Muslim. It is hoped that we shall soon have the last of the shame that is peculiarly Indian.'

At an individual level there was a strongly held kinship with others of the same faith that was preserved and promoted through intermarrying, shared histories, myths and customs. There was no such thing as one Muslim, Hindu or Sikh community in South Asia.

However, class acted as a social gel with Hindus, Muslims and Sikhs meeting together if they were rich, or if they were at the same university or if working on the land together. In 1945, there was no suggestion that 'mass slaughter' based on religion would happen.

The war had changed the country. 3 million had died in the Bengal famine of 1943. The 2½ million Indian soldiers who had served in the war with 24,000 killed and 64,000 wounded were returning, expecting their own country.

Politicians freed from prison were stoking up the hunger for independence. When Gandhi was freed from prison in 1944 with his ideology of non-violence, he seemed a figure from the past. Nehru and other Congress leaders were released in 1945. The Congress Party had changed since the 20s and 30s when it led mass protest against British rule and was now an umbrella organization for many ideas and politicians, such as committed Gandhians, liberals, socialists as well as Hindu nationalists. 'The system on indiscriminately enrolling four *anna* members has led to many forms of corruption and malpractices.'

Gandhi suggested that the Congress should be disbanded after Independence since it had achieved its stated purpose since 1929 of delivering *purna swaraj*, full independence. Gandhi's emphasis on spiritual development, self-sufficiency and village republics was at odds with Nehru's desire for a liberal, industrial and plural society. Without anchorage in Gandhian non-violence the nationalist movement was a much more volatile and dangerous proposition. The political 'isms' of the post-war world – communism, socialism, fascism and nationalism – were deeply felt as matters of life and death.

1946 started with a naval mutiny when ships in Bombay harbour trained their guns on the institutions of the Raj. Police mutinies in Bihar and Delhi followed, where policemen broke into their armoury. Anti-British protest movements followed in response. Congress Party politicians stoked the anti-British mood.

Armed resistance was against not only the British rulers but also the autocratic princes, with the peasants in up to 4,000 villages in Hyderabad rising in rebellion, supported by Communists.

British colonial officials found themselves disliked, overburdened and short of money. European civilians were abused but not harmed, whilst soldiers returning to Britain chalked on railway carriages: 'cheer, wogs, we are quitting India!'

Elections were called for the winter of 1945-6 with provincial governments elected to run provincial matters and a central body to draw up the future constitution of a free India. The Congress Party under Jawaharlal Nehru, forgetting its roots in Mahatma Gandhi's desire for freedom from imperialism through non-violence, was pitted against Mohammed Ali Jinnah's Muslim League, which demanded a separate Muslim country. The Congress Party claimed to speak for all Indians irrespective of religion; the League claimed to speak for all Muslims.

Posters and flyers spelt out their messages including 'Gandhiji and Jawaharlal Nehru are awakening us', and 'Pakistan: yes or no'. Tragically Gandhi's vision of non-violence and power devolving to the local communities was replaced by violence

The politicisation of religion became the order of the day

with *Fatwas* issued by all parties. Congress, too late as they had lost many of their Muslim supporters in the 1930s, would remind crowds that Gandhi opposed alcohol and usury – as defined by the Islamic law of the *Shariat*. The League tapped into the chauvinism towards unbelievers or *kafirs*, saying Congress was a cover for a Hindu party and suggested how one votes would be considered on Judgement Day. At the polling stations, political workers held up the Qur'an in one hand and Hindu holy texts in the other.

The result of the election, which was vitriolic and at times violent, showed the country polarised between Congress and League with the latter winning every Muslim seat. It was at this point that trust, the glue that kept the communities together, broke down.

By the autumn of 1946, massacres had started in a few states across India. In mid August the worst riots between Hindus and Muslims ever remembered broke out in Calcutta. Previously violence had been between political groups. Now the violence was targeted against innocent civilians, including women, children and the elderly. Jinnah called for a day of direct action to demonstrate support for Pakistan, speaking of Congress as a 'Fascist Grand Council'. This would show the strength of Muslim opinion and place him in a stronger position in future negotiations.

On the morning of 16th August advertisements were printed in Muslim papers. These were the headlines.

> Today is Direct Action Day
> Today Muslims of India dedicate their lives and all they possess to the cause of freedom
> Today let every Muslim swear in the name of Allah to resist aggression
> Direct action is now the only course
> Because they offered peace but peace was spurned
> They honoured their word but were betrayed

> They claimed Liberty but were offered Thraldom
> Now Might alone can secure their Right.

Handbills announced: 'In this holy month of Ramadan, Mecca was conquered from the infidels and in this month again a Jihad for the establishment of Pakistan has been declared.' The Mayor of Calcutta himself commanded: 'We Muslims have had the crown and have ruled. Do not lose heart, be ready and take swords. Oh *Kafir*! Your doom is not far and the greater massacre will come'. Huge portraits of Jinnah riding on a white horse and brandishing a scimitar were carried through the city.

Within three days, 4,000 Calcutta residents lay dead and 10,000 were injured. The political purposes of the riots are not in doubt. The Calcutta killings reinforced the idea that Hindus and Muslims were incompatible.

In October, 200 miles away in the East Bengal district of Noakhali a pogrom then took place when organised ethnic cleansing resulted in 5,000 rural Hindus being killed and women were forcibly converted and then often raped. Mahatma Gandhi arrived in November and stayed until March, preaching peace. Throughout India peace workers following the Gandhian line, found their job becoming almost impossible.

As if in revenge, Bihar, the mainly Hindu state next to Calcutta to the west, went on the rampage. Thousands of Muslims were killed. When Prime Minister Nehru visited the state, he was shocked to see on every house and every shop pro-Hindu slogans painted on the walls. He asked: 'All of you are shouting '*Jai Hind*' and 'Long Live Revolution'. What kind of country are you trying to build up?'

Across North India, rumour fed revenge and massacres followed. Refugees spread stories of atrocities, which added to the hatred between Muslim and Hindu. Even in far off Bombay, activists compelled Muslims to sign written denunciations of events in Noakhali. Trust between the two communities had broken down and people, fearful of their own security, were beginning to ask whether complete separation might be the only solution.

At the end of 1946, Gandhi wrote in his newspaper: 'We are not yet in the midst of civil war. But we are nearing it.' In the Punjab, the League, bypassed by coalition building in the state Assembly, waged a street campaign in the cities. On 24th January 1947, the Punjabi Government banned the Muslim League National Guard, but within a week it had retracted its decision indicating its weakness. Muslims and Hindus, who had previously been friends and neighbours, no longer greeted each other.

On 20th February 1947, Prime Minister Attlee, faced with problems nearer to home, such as a potentially bankrupt country, and involvement in civil wars in Palestine and Greece, announced in London that, by June 1948, India would receive its independence.

On 2nd March the premier of the Punjab resigned which marked the descent into civil war. Within the week, the major cities of the state, Lahore, Amritsar, Jullundar, Rawalpindi, Multan and Sialkot were burning.

Some Sikhs called for the division of the Punjab. Jinnah was continuously vetoing a united India and even Nehru, who later claimed that tired old men were running Congress, was starting to see Partition as a way out of the disaster facing the country. On the 8th March, the Congress Working Party accepted the possibility of the division of the Punjab.

On 22nd March the new Viceroy, Lord Mountbatten, flew in, and seized on partition as the solution to India's problems. He flew back to England and on 3rd June London announced a plan for partition.

Two weeks later Mahatma Gandhi declared: 'I do not consider Pakistan and India as two different countries. If I have to go to the Punjab, I am not going to ask for a passport.

And I shall go to the Sind also without a passport and I shall go walking. Nobody can stop me.' Sadly he would be wrong.

On 14th August 1947, ten months earlier than originally planned, partition came into effect, with the final boundary still not settled. The mass movement began and the massacres increased. It was Independence Day in Pakistan. Next day it was Independence Day in India. Mahatma Gandhi did not attend the celebrations.

On 30th January 1948 the divided country came partially to its senses when Mahatma Gandhi was assassinated in New Delhi. The assassin was a Hindu nationalist who opposed Gandhi's fasts for peace, his conciliatory policy towards Muslims and his peace overtures to Pakistan.

His death and the mourning that followed were observed not only in India but also in Pakistan. It led to a re-evaluation of the tragedy, which had overcome the sub-continent. Sadly the divisions were too deep. Initially Nehru was strengthened against the Hindu nationalists, but this lasted for less than two years. Partition in fact boosted the strength of the Hindu Right and relegated Indian Muslims to a difficult and precarious position in the early years of Independence.

CHAPTER 11
AMRITSAR AND THE SIKHS

Monday 6th August

Set in the middle of Amritsar's Golden Temple is a square pool. Worshippers are reading their holy texts 24 hours a day. Wonderful stones are laid into marble. In many places there is a restrained beauty, in others a blaze of gold and reds. Each section of the roof is a different shape.

Stepping on the threshold was not allowed. We are given delicious sacred foods to eat. Music is being played all the time – quite rhythmic and melodious – and poetry is being chanted.

The roof of gold leaf on copper cannot be looked at on a fine day. There is a door of silver on one side and ivory set in wood on the other. Thousands visit the Temple every day. The kitchen serves 2,000 free meals a day for all people.

The Sikh religion is the basis for brotherhood and tolerance. The Sikhs recognise women on an equal basis. Founded in the 15th century it is India's youngest religion.

Through a man who was a sergeant under the British – 'why not, of course' – we met a pioneer of the film industry in the Punjab. From a converted backyard of a studio and with a camera mounted on a home-made tripod, he had directed, written and starred in the most terrible film incorporating all the worst features of Hollywood in the most naïve way. The film was about modern gangsters but they still used swords! The good and bad men were very obvious. There was Rock and Roll in it plus romance – the lot! He was a very rich man and owned a whole street!

In the car ride from Amritsar the driver was very much against the partition and the bloodshed etc. He was full of talk about brotherhood etc. but it seemed a bit phoney when stopping to ask, in English, two Indians if they wanted help, then driving off before they could answer.

During our last ride into Delhi, we broke down about 3 times during the last 30 miles to our destination! We learnt money was kept for bribing the police – 90 rupees a time. There were checkpoints at the borders of all the states, to stop smuggling, check correct loads etc.

John's thoughts on the Sikhs

The third religious people of the Punjab, where the majority of the inter-communal massacres occurred at the time of the Partition, are the Sikhs. They were expelled from Pakistan Punjab.

In his diary Andrew mentions that he found the grave of Lt. Edwards, who conducted the siege of Multan in 1849. Multan had been part of the Sikh Empire since 1818. In April 1848, Lt. Herbert Edwards, a British Political Agent, had been near Multan but had been unable to save another Political Agent being murdered by a mob after taking possession of the fortress. On 22nd January 1849 the Sikh garrison fell to the East India Company, which led to the end of Sikh rule in March. For nearly 50 years, the Sikhs had ruled the Punjab from Lahore. The Sikhs' fighting ability was much respected by the British, who had fought them in numerous battles.

A less respectful sequel occurred on 13th April 1919 when the British Indian Army shot for ten minutes on a crowd of pilgrims in an enclosed garden near to their wondrous Golden Temple. Unable to escape from just five gates, perhaps 1,000 were killed in what became known as the Amritsar Massacre.

AMRITSAR AND THE SIKHS

It was in Amritsar, the spiritual home of the Sikhs, that I had my next awakening. Andrew in his diary describes the Golden Temple but to me, the Sikhs themselves were fascinating. Their welcome and hospitality were summed up in their belief in the equality of all beings, irrespective of their caste, creed, sex, nationality, and religion.

The Punjab, 'of the five rivers', was the birthplace of Sikhism. It contained a closely knotted Punjabi-speaking population of Hindus, Sikhs and Muslims, and was a vast recruiting ground for the British Army.

With the publication of the Partition Plan, trust between the three religious communities started to break down. As one anxious Punjabi wrote: 'May I bring to the notice of the Amritsar local authorities, that the people belonging to the various communities are losing confidence in each other because, among other things, of the big iron gates by which people are blocking off their streets.'

This resulted in a feeling of insecurity, with local politicians making the call to arms. Master Tara Singh who had already warned that Sikhs must be prepared to die for their cause, called for the formation of a Sikh army and stood defiantly brandishing his unsheathed kirpan on 3rd March 1947 on the steps of the Lahore legislative building, vowing: 'We may be cut to pieces but we will never concede Pakistan.'

Some Sikhs, however, called for the division of the Punjab, while in Amritsar a former newspaper editor started a campaign for a united Punjab. The Punjabi League leader and future Prime Minister of Pakistan, suggested that Sikhs should be incorporated as members of the new Pakistani Constituent Assembly, or that the Punjab's boundaries should be redrawn on linguistic grounds.

Sikh leaders who had miscalculated and urged Mountbatten to divide the Punjab, in order to limit Pakistan's extent and to save the whole province from Pakistani domination, now faced the unimaginable prospect of a severed community, with one half in India and the other half in Pakistan. The regions around Lahore, Multan and Rawalpindi, were dominated by Muslims but home to over half a million Sikhs, and the holiest Sikh pilgrimage sites, including Nankana Sahib, the 15th-century birthplace of the founder of Sikkism, Guru Nanak, fell in territory now labeled Pakistani. The Maharaja of Patalia told Mountbatten directly: 'the Sikh sentiment about this place is so strong that it would be most dangerous to minimize it, as under no circumstances can they be persuaded to allow this to go into a foreign country.'

The Punjab was now held hostage by volatile militia. In fear of a political backlash, the government of Punjab allowed well-known ringleaders to go free and British officials and Indian politicians wavered on the ban on weapons. Sikhs would be walking or cycling with very large kirpans. On 10th June a Sikh on a bicycle threw a bomb, left over from the war, into a horse-drawn cart carrying passengers in Lahore. Sikh leaders openly threatened an uprising to British officials and warned that a fight was inevitable if no heed was paid to Sikh solidarity.

Maps were being drawn to argue where the new border should be. A professor wrote to Jinnah with statistics showing administrative areas with Muslims in the absolute majority. He claimed that in Amritsar 'Muslims are less than the combined population of Hindus and Sikhs'. The Sikhs' memorandum to the Punjab Boundary Commission was 75-pages long.

A Lahore newspaper warned: 'To Sikh solidarity, the Mountbatten scheme will be what a knife is to a cheese piece: it will cut through it easily and definitely.' The Sikhs, a community of only six million, in an all-Indian population of almost four hundred million, became desperate. The Sikh population was almost evenly spread across the Punjab.

AMRITSAR AND THE SIKHS

What were the Sikhs to do now, with 'no homeland in the whole world except in the land of the five rivers'? They had lost their influence on the colonial state and felt their interests were being sacrificed on the altar of a broader constitutional settlement. They now demanded that the commission consider the rich regional Sikh heritage, their extensive landholdings and their architectural birthright including six hundred gurdwaras in Lahore, though here there was a narrow majority of Muslims, who would point out the city was the home of the formidable Badshahi mosque.

On 8th July over half a million Sikhs wore black armbands to signal their depth of feeling. They collected together in gurdwaras to pray for the continued unity of their community. Sikhs complained that their sons had died on the battlefields of Europe during two world wars and that this was how the British repaid them.

On 17th August, two days after Independence Day with the British Army in barracks or sailing away from Bombay, horrific inter-community massacres commenced. The close Sikh community in the Punjab was effectively destroyed.

Columns of refugees, 30-40,000 strong, created human caravans up to 45 miles long crossed between the two countries.

CHAPTER 12
DELHI, TEA WITH INDIRA GANDHI

Tuesday 7th August

I weigh about 128lbs on arrival in Delhi.

1st night – The beautiful aeroplane lights look like flashing insects.

We stayed in the Lakshmi Narayan Temple. We thanked the Sikhs in the visitors' book for what was actually Hindu hospitality! We were woken at 4.30 a.m. by the weirdest chanting.

In the morning we met a man in a bank in Delhi who was an extremist caste. He was a Brahmin. They included teachers, soldiers, merchants and labourers. Basically it was the only way to keep religion together. It was still very strong (we later found this to be untrue). He said British Rule was hated in India and it bled India white. In Burma, if Indians found an English soldier dying, they would cut his throat and drink his blood. Moslems were the most immoral race in the world. When 'beloved' talked about in Farsi it literally meant little boy who had never shaved. Thus they locked their women away for fear of perversion.

2nd night – We had dinner at the Youth Welfare Organisation. Invitations had been made to the Mayor of Delhi, Jagjivan Ram and Mrs Nehru. Beautiful music was played. We then spent the night with some Americans.

3rd day – We went swimming in the morning and then

DELHI, TEA WITH INDIRA GANDHI

visited the shacks of Dyal Singh School, which was co-educational! We listened to lectures.

There was a fiasco in the afternoon as we failed to keep an appointment with the President of Delhi University.

We had tea with Mrs Nehru and met a fabulous Indian girl who had been moved by D H Lawrence's 'Lady Chatterley'.

In the evening we went to a dinner party given by a dull English couple. We did the twist with the Americans.

4th day – We were up at 6.00 and I went to give a lecture to the Modern School, the equivalent of Eton, and answered questions. I received 50 rupees reward!

I was then shown round St. Stephen's College. Delhi University is exactly the same as Cambridge except that the teaching is done on a college basis – this is bad.

In the afternoon, I played a little golf and had an argument with some Japanese players. They told me to take a 3 iron for a shot needing the loft of a 5. I hit it straight into a tree. The caddy made me have another go with the 3, which I hit straight over the green, 100 yards from a fabulous American home. There were people living on the edge of a building site in cardboard boxes.

I take a taxi down Death Mile. The driver finds the road ahead blocked by buses so takes the right hand pedestrian path to get past. His speed started at 30 mph! A bullock cart was towing an old car.

5th day – We went for a swim in Ashoka, the biggest hotel in Asia. It had a typical European population. I then played golf with a playboy Indian Army polo player, who had 8 months leave a year!

I drive a car in Delhi, along Murder Mile where there are 365 deaths per year. A dog ripped up a postcard from home.

In the evening we went out with Lyne and Laurie to Motimahal and ate chicken tandoori. It was like lobster in looks but very good in taste and Indian. Then on to the Alps for dancing, which was very modern. There was no one else on the floor. My beard did not permit me to kiss anyone.

Andrew's memo from Delhi

Only 5 weeks since we left England and yet we are so far from home. The trip has been a wonderful success – the further east we go the more hospitality we receive.

The scenery changed from green to brown. Persia was 1,800 miles of unrelieved desert. The car gave way to camel long ago. If the countries have become less and less developed, the people have become kinder and kinder.

Here in Delhi we have been treated like kings and have even given lectures on our trip to important Delhi schools.

The Turks didn't cut us up. The Greeks didn't swindle us.

John's thoughts after tea with Mrs Nehru and Indira Gandhi

The high point of my visit to Delhi was my phone call to Jannie on her 20th birthday. Sadly she could only hear about one word in three and the Danish telephone operator kept on saying 'speak up'. She didn't even hear that I had bought her a present, a *shalwar kameez*. My memory of her was of a very, very slim girl of medium height. This did not help the sales assistant who was slim but not quite as tall. I suggested that the dress and the trousers should be made to fit her. Only when I reached Denmark did I find out that 'Indian' slim was far slimmer then 'European very slim'. Jannie at least fitted the slippers!

The next high point in my Indian adventure was also in Delhi. Andrew and I had tea with Mrs Nehru, who was the President of the Youth Welfare Organisation, whose reception we had attended the evening before. He had been given the above invitation by an Indian friend he had met at a Cambridge May Ball and with whom we were staying in Delhi. The guest of honour at the reception of the Youth Welfare Organisation was Jagjivan Ram, the Minister of Transport. He was India's first untouchable government minister. The photo on the back cover is of Andrew with a garland around his neck being introduced to the great man himself. A less bearded hitchhiker waits his turn.

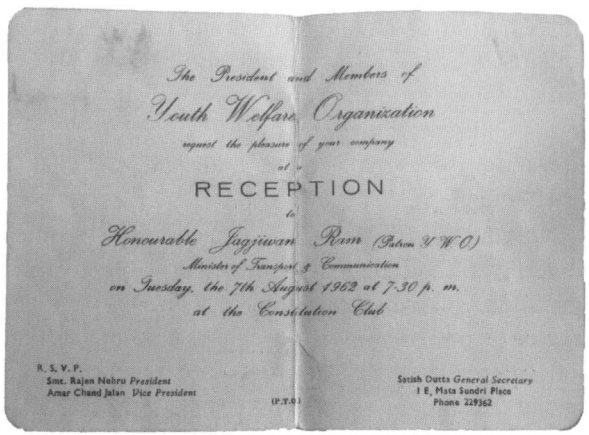

Whilst Andrew was chatting up a fabulous Indian girl, I was introduced to Indira Gandhi who was chief of staff for her father, Prime Minister Jawaharlal Nehru. She wanted her two sons, 17-year-old Rajiv and Sanjay, aged 15, to hear all about Cambridge University. She could not have chosen a worse example of that fine institution. Still, my salesmanship could not have been too bad as Rajiv took up an offer of a place at Trinity College. Sanjay studied automotive engineering and became an apprentice with Rolls Royce in Crewe.

In 1964 her father died and in 1966 she herself became Prime Minister. In 1975 she fell into a dispute with the Sikhs over who was the leader and who had the ultimate authority over the Sikh people: Guru Granth Sahib, the holy book of the Sikhs, or Indira Gandhi. At a major event to commemorate the 300th anniversary of the death of Guru Tegh Bahadur, when Indira Gandhi came onto the stage all rose to welcome her except Jarnail Singh Bhindranwale, which she must have felt was an insult.

Bhindranwale, 'the man from Bhindran', had called for a return to what is considered to be the 'pure' roots of Sikhism. As a religious leader, a Sant, he spoke against the consumption of alcohol and drugs and the laxness in religious practices, such as cutting the hair by Sikh youth rather than allowing it to grow naturally. He also strongly condemned the Indian constitution's Article 25, which declared minorities such as Sikh, Jains and Buddhists to be part of Hinduism.

In September 1981, after being accused of terrorism by the Government and the national media for his involvement in the murder of two supporters of a 'heretical sect', the Nirankaris, he turned himself in to the police but was released a month later after the Central Home Minister declared in Parliament that there was no evidence against him.

In August 1982, Bhindranwale and the Akali Dal party, which considered itself the principal representative of Sikhs, launched a movement based on the 1973 Anandpur Sahib Resolution, for a larger share of irrigation water, the return of Chandigarh to the Punjab and greater autonomy. Thousands joined the non-violent movement. He argued 'that neither must Sikhs oppress nor should they live under oppression'. He neither opposed nor supported the formation of Khalistan, a Sikh nation-state, and stated, 'we will not repeat the mistake of 1946, but we like to live together, we like to live in India.' However, he did consider Sikhs 'a distinct nation'. The law and order situation started to deteriorate. The Indian security forces killed many Sikhs, which led to the assassination of the Deputy Inspector-General of the Amritsar police in April 1983. It was at this point that Indira Gandhi should have arrested Bhindranwale and brought him before the law. Inter-communal violence escalated.

On the night of 5th October, Sikhs hijacked a bus and after separating out the Sikhs, killed six Hindus. Next day, Indira Gandhi imposed central government rule in Punjab, which was ineffective as the police were afraid of being shot.

On 15th December 1983, finding himself in danger of being arrested for threats he had made against some nationalist organisations, Bhindranwale moved to the Golden Temple. As Mark Tully wrote in *Amritsar, Mrs Gandhi's Last Battle*: 'All terrorists were known by name by the shopkeepers and the householders who lived in the narrow alleys surrounding the Golden Temple ... the Punjab police must have known who they were also, but they made no attempt to arrest them'.

Indira Gandhi first asked Lt. Gen. S. K. Sinha, then Vice-Chief of Indian Army and selected to become the next Army chief, to prepare a position paper for an assault on the Golden Temple. Lt. Gen. Sinha advised against any such move, given its sacrilegious nature according to Sikh tradition. He suggested the government adopt an alternative solution. A controversial decision was made to replace him as the Chief of the Indian army.

On 3rd June 1984, Prime Minister Gandhi initiated Operation Blue Star and ordered the Indian Army to raid the Golden Temple complex to remove armed militants from the complex. Bhindranwale was killed on 6th June, aged 37.

The use of artillery in the congested inner city of Amritsar proved deadly to many civilian bystanders living near the Golden Temple. Mark Tully was a member of the first press party to be escorted into the Golden Temple. In *India's Unending Journey*, he says:

'There were bloodstains on the marble pavements, and

the white walls were peppered with bullet holes. The library, containing invaluable manuscripts including copies of the Sikh scriptures, the *Gura Granth Sahib*, handwritten by some of the gurus themselves, was a charred ruin. But most shocking of all was the state of the Akal Takht, 'the throne of the timeless one', one of five takhts (seats of power) in the Sikh religion. The army had brought tanks into the precincts, crushing the marble pavement and pounding the shrine with squash-head shells. The whole frontage of the building had been blasted; every room seemed to be blackened by fire; and marble inlay and other precious decorations had been destroyed.'

Mark Tully and Satish Jacob criticized the army for burning down the Sikh Reference Library in *Amritsar: Mrs. Gandhi's Last Battle*, stating that this was done to destroy the culture of the Sikhs. In *The Sikhs of Punjab*, Joyce Pettigrew alleges that the army conducted the operation to 'suppress the culture, and political will, of a people'.

On 31st October 1984, Indira Gandhi was assassinated by two of her bodyguards, both Sikhs, in revenge for Operation Blue Star. This led to widespread killings of Sikhs in anti-Sikh riots.

Rajiv Gandhi succeeded Indira Gandhi and, by secret diplomacy rather than open warfare with the Sikh people, resolved the three major issues on which Bhindranwale had campaigned: Chandigarh was allocated to Punjab, with a commission ruling on border disputes; Punjab retained its share of water until a commission presided over by a judge decided on a permanent allocation; and the Anandpur Sahib Resolution, the statement of the Alkali Dal party in 1973, was sent to the one-man commission on centre-state relations set up by his mother.

CHAPTER 13
AGRA, AJANTA, ELLORA AND ON

Sunday 12th August

Our plan is to see the Taj Mahal by moonlight. We will spend the night in the grounds. This we learn is totally forbidden!

The 'Taj' is made of many different types of marble, of shades of watery grey and brown. Inside there is an octagonal screen of pure brown-coloured marble – beautiful intricate carving out of whole blocks – all around the white marble is inlaid with semi-precious stones in the shapes of flowers. Flowers constitute the majority of carvings. At night the light shone through the marble screen to reflect the most intricate and beautiful shadows on the two tombs.

The acoustics are fantastic. In the central chamber reverberations continue for 15 seconds. Even in the eight surrounding chambers they are very pure. The chambers are all different – very simple but beautiful with the same smooth marble floors everywhere. Everyone is in bare feet, some with most deformed legs and feet, some with pock marked faces. Many of the visitors seem to be peasants.

The whole looks like an ivory palace and should be isolated from everything else. In the middle gold, copper and bronze lanterns are hanging from the ceiling. They were presented by Lord Curzon. The incense smell is beautiful.

We sleep in one of the cloisters surrounding the 'Taj'. Next morning a guard wakes us. All we can say is 'we are students'!

Outside squatters sit on tables and sell their wares from their stalls.

Our first lift is for our baggage on a Sikh-powered handcart. Unfortunately our fitness wasn't up to the trot he broke into as soon as we had loaded up.

For our next lift John is hanging half in and half out of a cab during a monsoon shower.

From the rich land of the Punjab we move to the more barren palm-infested land south of Delhi.

Peacocks are common around Agra. We also saw a large monkey running wild. Sitting on the telegraph wires there is a bird, which sings like the hum of the wires. The bullocks are 90% submerged in dirty ponds.

Passed through the jungle north of Jhansi – my idea of Africa. We saw no tigers but they were there.

Planned letter to Indian Railways

Dear Sirs

The Jhansi Railway Room

The Jhansi central railway catering gave me a very poor impression today when I came here for the third time as a reminder for lunch. I, along with other senior Army retired officers of the UP Government were travelling to Bombay for attending the All India Seminar, but were held up because of the train.

The behaviour was very bad. An action with information to me as requested. They should know how to behave and attend the responsible persons and officers. Hope the same shall be improved in future.

At about 13.00 I came and called for one pot of tea along with pouched eggs etc. The tea given to me was prepared by dropping hot water over old leaves used by another person in the teapot used by him. When asked by me how it is done, your serviceman 3.20 spoke to me in an irresponsible way. I am much disappointed by such type of thing being done with the passengers, and when they are not supplied the desired good stuff in spite of paying in full.

I hope you will look in the matter, seriously.

Colonel Andrew Macalpine (retired)

John's card from Indore, India, 16th August 1962

Yesterday had first shower since we left Delhi 4 days earlier, from Negro to Paleface in one easy stage. But to add insult to injury we spent whole night lying on top of lorry carrying sheep and goats with torrential monsoon pouring down. We saw Taj Mahal at Agra – very impressive; although we spent night hidden beside it, the moon kept away so further enchantment was not possible. From there to Khajaraho and the temples of love. The eight temples we saw were covered with erotic sculptures and this alone was worth seeing for its artistic value, about 1,000 years old and truly magnificent. We move on to Bombay and we'll probably leave on 24th to be back in England 22nd September. All my love John.

Andrew's tall tales from the road

For 4 annas I asked for my boots to be cleaned by a shoeshine boy. His outraged and amazed laugh was infectious. I got it free in the end.

The bus-ride from Jhansi to Harpalapur was on a mud-shingle road. Bus travelling at about 50 leaves the road in avoiding a cow. It only stopped with the front wheels overhanging a stream having nearly tipped over. On the same bus we met a child who could recite perfectly but in almost incomprehensible English Wordsworth and Shakespeare. Both kids were Brahmin, aged 13 and 14 and very intelligent.

People were living from hand to mouth – happy by necessity.

The erotic temples at Khajaraho showed every intercourse position. No part of the body was left uncarved. Eroticism was everywhere but with much grace. The carving of the stone was if it was wood.

A woman with underfed baby in her arms was pregnant again.

The smell in the bus was like that in a farmyard.

Young children walk about naked.

Heavily laden ox was having a tug of war with its master – both remained stationary. In order to get the animal on the way he went to its rear and with a large stick thrashed its backside in different positions. A blow low down on its tail caused the animal to accelerate leaving master and load behind.

We tried a hitch on top of a bus but we were put inside for free – embarrassing when the bus was not stopping for peasants at the side of the road.

All women have enormous foot bangles, jewelled foot rings, and pierced left nostrils.

I had a great desire to clean my teeth and ironically I saw three people on the Harpalapur to Khajaraho road cleaning theirs.

A woman washed me at a well by pouring water over me.

Boys that look like girls are Sikhs with plaits which they keep until they are old enough to wear turbans. I couldn't understand their peeing position.

All the stalls are covered with corrugated roofing or large sheets of plaited bamboo. There are many sweet shops selling all kinds of pastries and sweet things!

Chess played in India is different to that we play in England: there is no castling, the queen is not on her own square, when the pawn reaches the other end you get a bishop not a queen, pawn allowed only one move at start, the white square is in the left corner. The people we played chess with bought us a meal and then came to the station to see us off at 4.30 a.m.

In the ladies latrine at the last stop before Jhansi, the occupants were a couple of goats.

A beautiful orange-leaved tree lines the sides of the road. In autumn it flowers and the flower is eaten by the poor and made into liquor by the rich.

Beautiful green parrots are seen in great flocks.

I met a Cambridge student on the train from Harlpalpur to Jhansi.

Coconut juice is fermented for two days and becomes Indian beer. It tastes like weak, flat, sour 'bitters'.

To make beetle-nut, two pastes are spread on a vine leaf, and then sprinkled with the nut. Everyone chews them as a digestive. They make the teeth and tongue etc. very red. Is this permanent?

Older men wear trousers, usually with one leg held up to knee length with elegant folds. They also wear long strips of cloth wrapped into circular turbans as opposed to the Sikh turbans.

The Indian 'way of life' is explained to us by an Anglo-Indian.

We compare earnings: a shunter on the railway or a mechanic earns about £2 or 25 rupees a week, a truck driver earns £7, a bricklayer or a master foreman earns 7 rupees a day whilst a small sweet shop owner's income is 2, 3 or 4 rupees a day. Cigarettes, even at 13d per packet of 10, are expensive.

I meet a woman looking like the dancing pictures. We have similar recreations: wireless, dancing and family.

Heat-stroke, especially on railways, is a problem.

The so-called problem of living since independence is probably a reflection on someone who can only earn £2 a week.

We see one of two Anglo-Indians drunk on coconut wine.

A donkey knocks over a bicycle in Jhansi.

We get a ride on a lorry carrying goats. It is packed very full and the smell is over-powering – it has no air-vents. Two of the goats are lying in urine at the bottom of the truck. One of the truck helpers went underneath the partition to sort the goats out. After a while, he reappears covered in goat shit.

I told a man in Jhansi that my watch cost 50 rupees - £4. They showed me theirs, which cost 100 and 110 rupees respectively and offered to swap.

Breasts are exposed with less and less coyness.

A flock of vultures are sitting on the skeleton of a cow. It reminds me of 'Suddenly Last Summer'.

Women are crapping at the roadside.

Judging by the population figures and number of houses there are at least ten people living in each house.

The petrol truck driver's attitude towards the occupants of small villages we passed through almost as uncomprehending as our own at the strange sights.

Having been caught by police with three in front of his cab, the driver bribed them 10 rupees. From then on, every time we arrived at a checkpoint one of us hid under the dashboard.

The locals' sense of decency is offended by my washing naked under the shower.

A Sikh's hair goes right down his back.

We see houses made of twigs and mud.

Buffalo horns grow in many different ways – usually useless.

We buy bananas from a banana grove for ½d each.

A woman's dress is an all red sari, with her waist bare.

The lift from Jalgvan to Ajanta and on to Aurungabad was carrying logs. There is trouble with the police who question the passengers. The driver must pay a 25 rupee deposit for his stupidity. The driver and mate then saw a sub-inspector.

AGRA, AJANTA, ELLORA AND ON

We saw monkeys in profusion at the edge of one village.

Indian music has much that is rhythmically similar to West Indian music.

We saw a real monsoon from underneath the 'Mac', or tarpaulin, on top of the truck.

A buffalo came to drink out of a washing-up bowl.

We found paradise at Aurangabad. Chai cost 7 n.p. (9d) and consisted of 3 teas, a large amount of jellabi and 2 butter balls.

The heat has an effect on the locals. The rain causes much dirt and temporary light entertainment for locals who either watch fascinated by the torrential downpour or, like the children, run through the streets laughing and soaking wet.

Beggars are a problem to be solved. There was a terribly deformed man in Aurungabad, with no feet, no hands and no nose. We gave him 10 n.p.

The editor of the Times of India etc. took to drink and is now eating pig-food!

Two Moslem friends had known each other for 8 years yet had never met each other's wives.

We ran out of sugar 30 miles from anywhere and stopped for a breather. On the horizon appeared a man on a bicycle. He came up and had 2lbs of sugar in a rag. Then he cycled off!

We met a man and his dog in an amphibian (Duck) in the middle of the desert.

We gave a man 2 shirts, so he puts both on.

We saw a Hindu funeral procession from the top of a bus. The girl being carried in the bier was garlanded with flowers. Her face was uncovered and looked if she was sleeping.

Ajanta and Ellora caves

The paintings in the Ajanta caves are in wonderful colours. All the emotions are expressed on the faces and all their positions show great grace. Women are glorified and are shown as things of great beauty. Tears and laughter are depicted with equal facility. There is no feeling of limitation of convention. Socks are worn, ladies' handbags are shown, a muffler and even a bowtie can be seen. There is a fantastic agonised expression on the man who is pulling out his own guts. There is great beauty of those around the 'Dying Princess', whose fingers are painted with exactitude and beauty. There is good use of perspective. Eyes, in particular, are wonderful. The whole consisted of enormous assembly halls and temples.

The carvings in the Ellora caves show grace in many figures, especially those dancing, in spite of much uniformity. The god Siva is begging for alms. The whole took many generations to finish. Beautiful green and blue parrots are making nests in the crannies of the rock half way up, where there is also a beehive. The honey is got out by poking a pole with a flaming cloth on the end and attached to a bucket. The fire chases the bees away, the pole pierces the wax and the bucket catches the honey.

A donkey to the rescue

As I fell into my usual restless sleep at the hard concrete base of the petrol pump I imagined that the next lift would see us into Bombay and thus close the chapter on our visit to India. I was to be proved wrong on both points.

I was woken at about 3 a.m. by what seemed to my semi-conscious mind to be the crying of a child in great pain. I sat up and witnessed an incident that must be counted extraordinary even by the standards of seasoned auto-stoppers.

For the last hour, John had been vainly attempting to wave trucks down. Of course the sophistication had long been abandoned and particularly now John was finding that the only way to arrest these speeding monsters was to stand in the middle of the road executing a frenzied twist-like dance as if his car and family had just crashed off the road in flames and the shock had demanded he should call for help immediately.

However these extreme tactics were proving not only in vain but extremely dangerous as the sense of power given to most drivers by their 'Mercedes' made them oblivious to everything on the road except those objects, which were immoveable such as walls or bridges, or bigger, such as buses.

Two things saved us capitulating to public transport. One was the alertness of the garage owner who had sensed for some time our predicament, the other was the presence of a donkey who, for the last hour, had been nibbling away at the rubber hose of the pump as if in deep and confidential conversation with the petrol gauge.

Suddenly and with cries of '*challo*', (come on, move) '*challo*', to the half-asleep garage attendants the owner made towards the offending animal with a look of pure enlightment in his eyes. With the obvious intention of moving the beast, they all started to beat it vigorously on its backside. However, it was no old wives tale, which likened stubborn people to mules and the effect of the thrashing on this particular animal was merely to produce a look of greater placidity on an already peaceful countenance.

Obviously the solution the owner had found to our problem was obviously not to be shelved so readily and, angered by the donkey's lack of response, all four of them made for the creature's head and started to haul him by the ears. Now there are few beings, human included, whose ears are not susceptible to such savagery and this creature was no exception.

A terrible braying, which incidentally woke me up, was accompanied by reluctant movement and the unknowing instrument of our next lift was led out towards the road. Until now John and I had been watching the scene incredulous but uncomprehending. We suddenly realised the reason for all the trouble and from bystanders we became willing participants in the sport. Six pairs of hands on two ears was perhaps unfair but extremely successful and in spite of the donkey's unbalanced sensitivity where equal pressure on both ears would result on him describing a circle in an anti-clockwise direction, our temporary captive was positioned after many circles on route in the middle of the road where, our grip having been released and all encouragements to move gone, he remained motionless like some tribute to the statue-like qualities of his race.

The scheme's greatest test had yet to come and the six of us waited at the side of the road to watch the results of our work. We had not long to wait before we heard the roar of the first truck preceding it through the still night air. Sounds carry for great distances under such conditions and our nerves were taut with apprehension by the time the great motor's headlights swung round the bend 300 yards up the road. Although the truck was travelling fast the powerful beam soon picked out the still motionless four-legged road island. His dilemma must have started for on the narrow road there were only two solutions: to drive on hoping the donkey would move; or stop.

Fortunately this particular driver must have suddenly remembered something his grandmother told him about the stubbornness of mules for, having looked like driving straight on, he applied his brakes at the last minute and came to a noisy halt a couple of feet from the obstruction.

A few words from the garage owner to the truck driver concerning our predicament: 'London to Bombay', 'student with no money' and we were bundled into the back having thanked the garage workers profusely for their troubles. The donkey meanwhile had been forgotten and just as we were about to drive off, it was noticed that it was still standing motionless two feet from the lorry's bumper. Once again eight hands grabbed two ears and after much braying the road was cleared and we drove off.

Our travelling companions for this, the penultimate lift on our great journey, were a few thousand bananas and a large number of rats, which we could hear scampering around in between the double layer of canvas above our heads. In fact, we could see nothing as the canvas at the back of the lorry had been firmly lashed down and it was fortunate that neither of us had claustrophobic tendencies as the darkness was very dense.

The first thrill of being packed in with such delicious fruit was shattered as the bananas were far from being ripe and thus very hard to sit upon. Worst of all, however, was the sharp splintering crack, which greeted every movement and told us another handful of precious fruit had been irrevocably torn from its stem. The most insensitive of men could not have hidden from himself some feeling of guilt at such flagrant waste.

We kidded each other about the dreaded Tarantula but fortunately no such hairy monster came to plague us and I imagine some boyhood misconception led us to associate them with bananas.

During the course of this ride the driver made many stops and some indication of his feelings could be gathered from the fact that not once did he release the canvas, not necessarily to offer us a cup of the chai, which he was liberally indulging himself (why else do people stop?) but just to give us the momentary relief of a shaft of light or breath of air. When eventually the canvas was released at one of the numerous stops we rightly supposed that it presaged our departure rather than refreshment.

Tuesday 21st August

We had only a few minutes roadside vigil before St. Christopher manifested himself again and we found ourselves travelling the last 50 miles into Bombay in company of a convoy of Sikhs. The end of any succession of events designed to please should leave a pleasant taste in the mouth and what proved to be our last piece of hitching satisfied this need in every respect. The convoy consisted of three Mercedes trucks all travelling very fast who amused themselves by overtaking each other when they had exhausted other competitors.

It must have been a Monday because about 30 miles from Bombay all three lorries stopped and it was soon obvious that they were set to do their weekly wash in the nearby mountain stream. Like naughty schoolboys freeing themselves from the restraints of uniforms they unwrapped their turbans and threw off their shorts.

Modesty, of course, prevents them undressing further and they always retained the towel-like cloth around their loins. It always strikes me as paradoxical that men who exhibit as few inhibitions amongst themselves as the Indians – they seem unable to forbear to handle each other when talking and to see two men walking down the street in Bombay holding hands is as common occurrence as it is in Iran – that men who show so little restraint in their day-to-day physical relations should fall short of an act that even the most conventional of Europeans would consider normal – namely exhibiting one's naked body before friends.

However, there was no checking their enthusiasm once in the water and it was easy to see why Sikhs have produced such soldiers and athletes as we watched these lithe bodies fighting each other with sure footed ease in the small rapids where both John and myself had difficulty in standing up. The stream itself was surprisingly cool and the explanation for this may not be difficult to find for towering up behind us was a most beautiful mountain completely blanketed by thick tropical greenery and shrouded at the top by a light mountain mist it seemed to possess some mysterious secret and it came as no surprise to learn that the mountain was in fact the sacred home of one of the Hindu gods. This piece of information came from a particularly well-dressed Indian who appeared like HG Wells' time traveller to come from nowhere.

The washing and bathing having been completed we climbed back into the lorries and sped off once again towards our destination. This time John and I were each travelling with a different set of drivers and I was unfortunate enough to be landed with the hungry couple – particularly so as we had not eaten for 24 hours. I found the only way I could tolerate the ordeal was to turn my back on their voracious appetites and immerse myself in conversation with a huge Sikh (it seems they stick together much as the Jews do) who was the proprietor of the small eating-house. Having ascertained I wasn't German he started talking about the war and was delighted at my imitation of English and Indian forces combining in the form of a cup and saucer on one knee to sweep Hitler in the form of a spoon off the other knee.

John's thoughts on rural India

Andrew's diary brings back the excitement of two young men travelling through a friendly but alien country. My one other memory, which Andrew never recorded, was hitching along some remote country road. From the hill above we saw a politician leading his followers down towards us. This almost biblical sight was so far from the politics of England and the empty village hall meetings. For the much criticism we met over the partition, Britain had at least bequeathed India a vibrant democracy.

CHAPTER 14
BOMBAY AT LAST

Wednesday 22th August

A few miles out from Bombay we crossed the stretch of water, which separates the city and its surrounds from the mainland of India. Looking back on our visit I am glad of this because Bombay was so completely divorced from the impression I had gathered of the India we had fleetingly glimpsed in the two previous weeks.

My first illusion about the great seaport was soon shattered, namely that it was as someone had so vividly described – compact. Many miles from the centre the struggle of huts and stalls started with every now and then a large factory glowering drably and smokily over the squalor. These rounded huts made of thatch with roofs like coolies' hats were, I later learned, an integral part of the Bombay housing scheme as was made quite clear by an educated but very poor Goanese woman I spoke to later on. She was seriously considering buying one of these crude shelters not having enough money for anything else.

Our first task, as always when we entered a city was to find somewhere to stay. Our resolution to spend at least one night in a hotel and really rest our aching limbs was soon broken and it was not long before we were led off to one of the two Sikh temples in Bombay. If ever my impressions were used in evidence as an indictment against the city, the case for the defence could put himself in a strong position by pointing out that we were quartered in one of the most squalid areas. Anyway at the time a Sikh temple seemed only one step removed from a cheap hotel and of course it was free!

Even if we were not expecting the magnificence of the Hindu temple in New Delhi, the unpretentious doorway, which greeted us – no more, no less – seemed to promise something rather less comfortable than the cell we had under the other religion. The temple was located in the dock area and thus the slum area. The fruit peel from the nearby stall, which was scattered around the pavement in open defiance of the basket clearly marked for 'Refuse', was the most immediate indication that we had come a long way from the attempted hygiene of New Delhi.

Our lodgings were on the first floor of the building we entered and the pungent odour of filth which lingered obstinately around the foot of the staircase seemed to breathe a warning to us to get as high above ground as possible and away from not only the smell but the prostrate bodies lying awkwardly on broken pieces of stone like dumb guardians of some lower world hidden deep in the recesses under the staircase.

At the top of the staircase, which rose straight from the street, stood a small table and all around we could see bars behind which on both sides ran a veranda encircling both houses for it now appeared that the stairway had been built between the houses and was used as a communal entrance to the respective gates on the first floor. At the table sat our panel of judges for admission to this heaven – three bearded Sikhs ready to expel Satan himself and more than ready we felt to turn their heads from the beggarly cries of two hitchhikers. However, our apprehension was baseless and three wide grins greeted our anxious looks and soon, particulars having been taken, we were being shown our own and everyone else's quarters.

This was not difficult as the whole consisted of one stone-floored room about 40 feet long and 30 feet wide and walled by many dilapidated wooden lockers sporting a great variety of different locks. The number of sleeping and dozing bodies we discerned in all parts of the dimly lit room at an hour when most people were working suggested that by night time there would be much overcrowding and yet we soon found out that most of the occupants of the temple spent the days in greater and lesser states of somnambulance.

Woke in the Sikh Temple to beautiful sad music. Bombay is stinking with money and dirt. There is terrible dishonesty amongst the many moneychangers and street vendors. Nude children are running around and we saw women peeing outside the post office. The squalor and poverty is everywhere, so many are struggling for existence. There are an enormous number of beggars.

We met people emigrating to Australia who had spent eight months on their trip and were trying to sell their bus for 6,000 rupees (£480).

We watched the Hindu Festival for Krishna, the God. Rabbles were dancing and flute playing round the streets of Bombay. Formations of human pyramids reached up to pots of money suspended across the roads. The burnt sandalwood makes a beautiful smell.

A man with a huge grin followed us around. He wore beautiful Sunday clothes. We stopped outside a brothel and drunks were tumbling down the stairs into taxis and back up again. We were eventually offered a sari-clad girl – not terribly attractive.

We saw our first snake charmer, with three cobras in baskets. He had a flute and drum but was most unexciting. Obviously he was not afraid of snakebite. An English tourist gave 2 rupees to take 2 photos.

On our last night we saw the successful Hindi film *Gunga-Jumna*. There was superb photography and some good acting but like all Indian films it was a fully-fledged musical so that scenes of the utmost drama were interspersed with current hit songs. The attempt to introduce every facet of cinematic art, western, love, rape, drinking etc. had something in common with the work of the director we met in the Punjab. I spent the whole evening clutching my newly bought leopard skin!

We met the French director of the French merchant shipping company *Messageries Maritimes* who told us about the terrors of travelling third class on an Indian boat: 'You know many of the people are coloured!' So we booked on the *MS Dumra* with the British India Steam Navigation Company, which can accommodate 1,537 deck passengers, and has 20 First Class or 30 Second Class cabins, bound for Khorramshahr, Iran.

John's letter from Sikh Temple, Bombay, 22nd August

Salam old sport,

Shukria for letter. After 3 weeks in India I am pidgin English and pidgin Hindi. This morning I received apology for being bad Danish girl. You are forgiven darling.

In reply to your sincere question about my existence, I have not withered away yet, but at this rate it won't be long. Minimum fare to Europe is £63 to Marseille and £80 to UK. And so we are probably going lowest class in an Indian junk to Iran and from there hitching or bussing home. If all goes well I arrive in Denmark 20th September. Would you send mail to ISTANBUL or MUNICH. Whatever happens can I receive a short note in MUNICH saying whether invitation is still on.

Bombay is really poor and beggars are everywhere. We are living at above address and it is said that to sleep on the balcony is safer than in the only room. Inside there are large bugs – outside only mosquitoes as the bugs are washed away in the monsoon. However, monsoons finished officially two days ago. (This did not prevent the heavens letting rip on us poor mortals below yesterday.) When it's 95°F (35°C) here it's cool. This seems like a fairy tale but between you and me the Indian thermometers are wrong.

Re. Beards. Andrew spent 6d and had his trimmed – hence none left. I cannot afford 6d and feel that if the man did trim my effort there would be none left (as there wasn't much before). And so I grow my 97 ginger whiskers in anticipation of wee goatee on left foreside of face (near chin).

I have spent 3 days buying 2 presents. Mum is receiving a chunk of hewn silver in the form of a bracelet. Since silver is 4 times as cheap here as in England it is a good buy and I am sure she will like the present. Yours is not a secret. If you do not measure 34-23-35 you had better change your figure.

My dear Jannie, you will have a real Punjabi *shalvar kemis* to wear if I arrive in Denmark. It is fabulous and needless to say both Andrew and I have a great desire to try it on! However we are statistically slightly wrong. As a sari is so hard to wear and this is the most fabulous fashion I have plumped on the Punjab national costume. I spent the day with the tailor and we have arrived at a compromise. If I can get some Rajhistan slippers as well you will be the beat girl of Hellerup.

Only other news is about hitching as all my deep philosophies can wait. This is an A1 hitching story. Whilst Andrew slept, I hitched. 6 trucks went by – reason it was two in the morning and I look a real rogue now. By 3 I was desperate. Large commotion nearby and I see garage hands (who never seem to sleep) assaulting donkey who had been sucking end of petrol pump. Jo (donkey's name) is dragged by ears (2 men on each ear) to middle of the road. Truck comes, Jo stays, truck stops, and we are off to Bombay. How about that?

I'll keep writing like a faithful slave – if you feel extra keen a card in Tehran, Iran would be fabulous. Anyway, my darling fiancée, looking forward to seeing you around 20th September.

All my love John.

John's card from Bombay, Friday 24th August

Still Bombay. However we sail on Sunday for Persian Gulf – in unberthed class! This is usually for Asians but we have shown how tough we are and saved much money. Do you know what a tandoori chicken looks like? Well, it looks just like me – pink all over. Over dose of tropical sun has turned me into a lobster. For the last few days many hours have been spent discussing yogi – and god realisation – both subjects, which I feel strongly about. It has been a great change from answering the three standard questions, which everyone has learnt in English. I hope *bror* is still collecting stamps. [There are 8 stamps on the front of the card]. All my love John.

CHAPTER 15
HOMEWARD UP THE
PERSIAN GULF

Sunday 26th August

Every conceivable activity is taking place on this boat from the deck games of the Second Class passengers to the begging of an old bead-bedecked peasant. The ship even had its red-light district. One beggar, with form, had his ticket bought by a rich man with a harem.

There is even a stowaway in our midst – a black longhaired ape like man. (I first saw him swinging down from one deck to the other.) He certainly looks more content than some of his fellow Indians. Yet it is in his deep dark eyes that his story can be read: the death of his parents in Bombay when he was 15 and subsequent emigration to Pakistan and Karachi, where he stayed for the next 10 years.

A cock crowing woke us up each morning.

Little shops were set up by Arabs travelling one or two ports just for the business. There was a great emphasis on men's cosmetics. Fruit was sold. Many of the Arabs bring their own food: chicken, meat, flour etc. and cook in one of the galleys especially for the purpose.

Many of the about 800 deck passengers hang curtains around a small area of deck and construct their own tent, where they live like nomads in the desert. People were sleeping everywhere, including one couple in a lifeboat!

There are numerous cocks and hens on board.

Knifings are frequent. One surly Iranian received a gash on his ass from a Baluchi. 4 years ago one officer was killed, another paralysed and two more wounded in a fight. There was usually a fight in the galleys at each sitting.

Last year, the sister ship *MS Dara* sank off Dubai after a bomb explosion occurred between decks. 239 passengers, crew and shore personnel died. Ten trunks were thrown down on top of the Chinese lifeboat operator.

Much gold smuggling was going on. Packets are thrown off the ship and picked up by fast launches.

Handcuffs were much in evidence. One man in handcuffs walked around the ship but nowhere to land. An immigration officer comes on board, falls asleep and becomes a stowaway.

A Somali friend, who was going to show us round Kuwait, spoke of Arab impetuousness and hot-headedness, where a fight could be started over the most trivial incident and easily lead to a killing. A harsh English judge came to Aden and dealt out long sentences for all sorts of physical violence and stopped much of the bloodshed due to ignorance and lack of education where man never learns the difference between right and wrong.

The heat was so great that it seemed that little beads of perspiration were appearing on the surface of the water.

On a positive note, our deck considered making a collection for us.

John's card from on board *MS Durma*, Karachi, Thursday 30th August

This certainly has been great sport – underneath the awnings on the stern deck – Arabs, Persians, Baluchis, Pathans and 2 Englishmen (that's us). The big trouble is the diet – only Indian food. However, we'll survive the nine days and then it's a sprint home. By now you must think I'm nuts sending envelopes of stamps. I just hope the brother has still got room for more. [There are 11 stamps on the front of the card]. The sea is healing up the wounds of battles with lorries and although the temptation is to lie through the days we have some interesting places coming up: Muscat, Bahrein, Kuwait and others in the Persian Gulf, which seems very romantic.

See you soon. All my love, John.

John's card from Kuwait, Thursday 6th September

The card shows an Arab holding a falcon. Mohammed Ferdosi himself (alias John Waller). Arabs are a great giggle. On an average one knifing each day. Last trip 18 stowaways found. Unberthed quarters are any hole in the ship, lifeboats or holds. However, we have had a great frolic with our bed-mates, who play whist and sleep with monstrous daggers under their pillow. For the last 6 days we've been visiting Sheikhdoms along the Persian Gulf doing a ferry service: Muscat, Oman; Dubai; Qatar; Bahrein; Kuwait. This is a great country of Cadillacs and camels. Cannot wait to see you old sport. Arrive probably 20th. All my love, John.

John's thoughts on the Gulf

Andrew's diary portrays the primitive existence we lived on board the *MS Dumra*. I remember that tea was free before some early hour of the morning. By sucking in air at the same time as drinking the boiling beverage, I was able to down vast quantities. This technique provided me with an asbestos mouth.

In 2014, we visited some of the ports in the Persian Gulf we had seen in 1962. I looked in vain for the names of the ships painted by sailors on the cliffs as one enters exquisite Muscat.

HOMEWARD UP THE PERSIAN GULF

Dubai had obviously changed out of all recognition in the 50 years that had lapsed; I promised Jannie one of the great experiences of my hitchhiking through Iran: sleeping a tranquil night under the stars in the desert. Unfortunately we camped under the flight path into the International Airport.

Abu Dhabi's name means 'father of the deer', which we were told came from Irish sailors shipwrecked on the island, who, desperate for water, found a deer instead. What a wonderful tourist tale as the deer then led them to water.

In 1962 we carried on up the Gulf to Bahrain and Qatar before landing in Kuwait and then continued up the Shatt-al-Arab, passing the oil terminal and refineries of Abadan, one of the world's largest, to Khorramshahr. In 1980 Saddam Hussein saw an opportunity to become the dominant power in the Gulf with the perceived weakness of Iran after Khomeini's 1979 revolution. He invaded Iran over the 'Arab River', destroyed the Abadan refineries and, from September 22nd until November 10th, fought for the city of Khorramshahr, which became known in Iran as the 'City of Blood'. Over 7,000 lives were lost on both sides. The Iranians recaptured the city in May 1982. Two months later, after an unsuccessful attempted invasion of Iraq, Khomeinei had an opportunity to sue for peace. The Iranian Revolutionary Guard however persuaded him that on religious grounds he should continue into Iraq as 'the road to Jerusalem passes through Karbala'. The war ended in 1988, by which time over a million Iranians had lost their lives, as martyrs, and between a quarter and a half million Iraqis had been killed.

Karbala, 350 miles further up the Euphrates, is the symbolic city in the great Shia/Sunni divide, which started when the Prophet Muhammad died. His father-in-law Abu Bakr rather than his cousin and son-in-law Ali succeeded him. The Shias were the 'partisans of Ali' whilst the Sunni were the followers of the *Sunnah*, the customs and traditions of Muhammad.

In the 61st year of the Islamic calendar (680AD), Muhammad's grandson Husein ibn Ali was killed by forces from the Umayyad caliph in the Battle of Karbala. Imam Husein is the supreme martyr of Shia Islam.

In 1744 the religious Imam Muhammad ibn Abd Al-Wahhab joined forces with the warrior Prince Muhammad ibn Saud to form the First Saudi State, which, in 1802, sacked the holy Shia city of Karbala and destroyed the tomb of Husein ibn Ali. It is now a geo-political as well as religious divide, so fundamental that there seems to be no solution.

Two years later in 1990, Saddam would attack Kuwait on the pretext that it was stealing its oil and keeping the price low in order to throttle Iraq's recovery from the war against Iran. This led to the First Gulf War.

In 2003, the US and British invaded Iraq in the Second Gulf War and overthrew Saddam Hussein, leading to the country's occupation.

In 2011 the minority Sunni ruler of Bahrain put down an uprising in support of the demand for greater human rights with help from forces from Saudi Arabia and UAE. As punishment 35 Shia mosques were destroyed.

We knew little back in 1962 about the tension between the Sunni and Shia worlds. We were more involved in the pleasures of travel with Arab and Persian passengers, whom we played cards with on deck and who wanted to make a collection for their new friends.

John's card from Harbiye Gurdu, Istanbul, Friday 14th September

This morning we crossed over the Bosphorus into Europe. We have made fantastic time since we arrived in Iran as we have been roughing it on 3rd class trains for most of the way. The slow trains are half the price as the express and the only difference being that the former stop at every station – every 10 miles – whilst the express stops at alternate stops.

To be back in a cooler climate is great but we both had a dose of the 'flu – temperature 39°C. This can be expected as in the Persian Gulf the temperature in the shade went up to 45°C each day. Green trees and cool water is a glorious change.

I should arrive in Hellerup on the 19th. However, once I get to Copenhagen, I'll phone and then come on over. I was furious with you this morning as there was no letter here but you've 5 days to think of an excuse. Perhaps though I'll race this card. There may be an outside chance of my arriving in the evening of the 18th or, if visas cause trouble, the morning of the 20th (as promised in Bombay). Don't worry, I promise to be clean but sharpen your scissors and have some disinfectant ready as the bed bugs love me and the Indian ones sure hold on. Perhaps today, I'll cut my beard off. All my love John.

John's thoughts on his last leg to Denmark

It was time for our race for home by the fastest and cheapest means possible. Andrew would be returning for his final year at Cambridge, on his way to become a great teacher, a head master and a teacher of head masters. I would start work as a trainee systems engineer at IBM. By train and bus we retraced our journey via Tehran and Istanbul. We parted in Belgrade, Andrew travelling on by train to London and I by train to Munich from where I planned to hitchhike to Denmark to see Jannie.

Outside Munich station, I watched a large German buy a whole cooked chicken to eat. Being a skinny starved traveller, I saw a challenge and also bought a chicken, which barely fitted into my shrivelled stomach. The game was lost as he ordered and ate a second chicken. My Indian friends would have been shocked.

In a Mercedes, on the autobahn somewhere in Germany, I realized my host, a bald immense man, and I had a problem – a language problem. I had exhausted my examples of *gut* and *nicht gut* and we sat in silence for kilometre after kilometre. Suddenly he grinned and announced, '*Adenauer lieber De Gaulle.*' Konrad Adenauer was the German Chancellor and Charles De Gaulle was the French President, the leaders of two peoples that had been enemies for nearly a hundred years, fighting three wars in which millions had died. On our great journey, we had travelled through discredited empires. I now realized that we were entering a new phase for a united Europe, one of peace and hopefully prosperity. I vowed that, with a passion, I would be involved in this great adventure.

Now I was on my way to Denmark to seal my own European Union. My last lift dropped me on Copenhagen's ring road and I started my short walk up Bernstorffvej, before turning into CVE Knuths Vej. I had made a call from a telephone box soon after I had started my walk, so a welcoming party was walking coming down the street. Jannie could barely believe this bearded man was still alive. Her moustachioed father was such a wonderful man he later wanted to drive me for many kilometres rather than let me hitch back to England, her exceptionally beautiful mother rather fell for me, her friendly brother liked his stamps and her young sister became my Danish teacher. Jannie herself waited 18 months before giving in to a boyfriend who hitched once a month from London to Copenhagen, with an expertise learnt on his epic trip.

CHAPTER 16
INDIA FIFTY YEARS ON

I have always wanted to travel back in time and witness the India of 1962. Having lost my camera in Turkey, we now have no record of what was still essentially a rural country.

To celebrate 50 years of marriage, in 2014, Jannie and I took a 4-month P&O cruise to the Far East. On our way home, we stopped off at four ports in India, which re-awoke my love for this wonderful country.

On Tuesday 11th February, 2014, we stopped off at the Andaman Islands, which was settled by Christian and Hindu refugees from East Pakistan at the time of the Partition. Previously it had been a penal colony to which freedom fighters had been sent and incarcerated in the Circular Prison of Port Blair. P&O was offering three excursions: Port Blair Highlights – a visit by coach to the prison where Mahatma Gandhi (it was wrongly claimed) was imprisoned by the Brits; Port Blair by rickshaw – a visit by rickshaw to the prison; or Rubber, Spice and Local Life. No contest. We go for Rubber, Spice and all things nice, which is the underdeveloped India out of the town. The passengers who stay in town are unhappy as it is very poor and most of the shops are stalls for locals or building material. (This sounds like 1962.)

Our guide hasn't a mike so he stops the bus every time he wants to say anything. At first he was incomprehensible as the local accent is worse than the worst curry house Indian but spoken very quickly. He makes up for the deficiency by waving his arms like a conductor. But after a while, we pick up enough words to interpolate the missing ones and all is OK. 'We have no crime, no drugs and no beggars.' 'Japs came in 1941 for 4 years. British get off island.'

There are many *tuk-tuks*, 3-wheel scooters used as taxis; all motorcycle drivers wear helmets but none of their passengers do; women wear the *shalwar kameez* and have long pony tails; everyone waves and there is the sunny feeling of the Bahamas, but here it's hilly rather than flat. The buildings and walls are all whitewashed.

Signs are in English: 'Save Water', 'Tuberculosis is completely curable', 'You are entering an accident-prone area', 'Do not litter'.

We see only one Hindu temple during the day but plenty of evidence of Christianity: Mercy Mission Church, Pentecostal Mission Church and a Catholic School.

The countryside is interesting: a man with a hand sickle cuts the field, solitary goats are tied by a rope to restrict them to eating a grassy patch, cows are everywhere – it is India. The palm trees are now very dense. 80% of the island is jungle and elephants are used to drag trees and take children to school.

The road, the Great Andaman Trunk Road, is narrow and very bumpy and the bus has no suspension. We sit on the back seat and the ride is very painful. We slow down for oncoming traffic and twist and turn round numerous corners and climb up and down small hills. Little houses hide in the forest – this is such a lovely place.

We drive on to the local school and cause a traffic jam. We can't get past a parked bus whilst a car and a bus are coming in the other direction. We can't back as a car on 'vaccination duty' and a motorcycle are behind us. What drama! The school is pre-school until grade 8. The boys and girls at the school are delightful and two of the male teachers explain that, though they are Hindu and Muslim, there is no friction between religions on the islands.

INDIA FIFTY YEARS ON

Andrew, the future educator, would have been in his element. Above each classroom there was a plaque with words of wisdom inscribed:

- Take pride in how far you have come. Have faith in how far you can go.
- If you cannot do great things, do small things in a great way.
- Tears and smiles make the music of life.
- If you give me rice I'll eat today; if you teach me how to grow rice, I'll eat every day.
- The roots of education are bitter, but the fruit is sweet – Aristotle.
- There is no substitute of hard working.
- Try not to become a man of success but rather try to become a man of value – Albert Einstein.

Another school displays its mission: 'Our school mission is committed to preserve Telugu Cultural Heritage and provide capabilities to students for achieving their potential to adapt and adjust to a diverse and ever changing society'.

The unwritten message to development aid-averse residents in England: 'We should count our blessings and be proud that our country can help the education in the poor third world!'

What a lovely day we have had. It brings back memories of our time in India. The people were a delight.

On the 3rd April 2014, we stopped at Cochin, which brought back memories of litter and hustlers. The conversation went: 'Only five dollars . . . but I would accept four . . . three dollars is as low as I will go . . . do you want it for just two dollars?' The answer was that Jannie and I didn't want it anyway. Andrew would have been in his element and bought it for two annas.

I read in Barbara D. Metcalf and Thomas R. Metcalfe's

HITCHHIKING TO INDIA IN 1962

A Concise History of India: 'In the 1967 election, the Communist party in Kerala came to power. From this time onwards, though poorly favoured with resources, Kerala embarked on a development scheme of its own which made it by the end of the century the one Indian state with near universal literacy and effective gender equality of men and women'. 'The far south western state of Kerala, though not a leader in per capita income growth, has sustained quality-of-life indicators, such as gender ratios, literacy levels and population growth rates, not far short of those found in first world countries.'

On the 4th April 2014 we visited Mangalore. I wrote: 'Today we will travel inland for an hour and a half and I hope to relive the great hitchhike to India in 1962 with Andrew. My theory is the country roads of today will resemble the main roads of 1962'. Our tall guide, Rohan David Fernades, who I guessed correctly was a fast bowler in his youth, suggests that the roads have been little changed for 60 years, when it was asphalted and then just wide enough for two trucks to pass, though sometimes with wheels on the verge.

Our journey along National Route 66 is progressing well through hilly, forested countryside. We meet an ancient truck crossing a single-lane British-built steel bridge over a river. I feel like getting out and hitching a lift. I wonder if it was driven by a Sikh? In 2014, pleasant houses are set in the trees and there is no sign of poverty in the countryside. *Tuk-tuks,* known as auto-rickshaws in India, race along, even overtaking the coach at one point, with a fanfare of tooting. The horn is used continuously to warn the vehicle ahead that one wants to pass and then again as the dangerous manoeuvre is performed. Police roadblocks had been set up at regular intervals along the route to halt potential political paymasters. Election law forbids bribery and there was a general election campaign in progress. The police were looking for large sums of cash. The Congress Party lost the election because it was seen to be corrupt.

Jain, however, is the real mystery to be solved. This ancient religion, still practised around the world by usually rich people, such as the diamond traders of Antwerp, but now in serious decline in India, has two glorious places of worship deep into the rolling countryside. Jainism has no gods only liberated souls, the 24 propagators of their faith known as *tirthankara*, with Adinatha as the first and Mahavira as the last of the current era. For a long time it was the state religion of India but it has dwindled, like Buddhism, over time by the growth of Hinduism and Islam with less than 1% of the population now being Jains. They are extreme vegans, not eating anything grown below the ground such as potatoes, onions and garlic as, by digging these up, worms and insects could be harmed. They have the highest degree of literacy in India at more than 94%. Many of their adherents are wealthy and support educational institutions. The Jain community is divided into two major sects, one where the monks do not wear clothes and the other when they do. Their belief in non-violence is the strongest in any religion and they vow always to tell the truth. 'Attempting to extort material wealth from others or to exploit the weak is considered theft.' Yet their occupation was traditionally in money lending! Jains postulate that the universe was never created, nor will it ever cease to exist. It is independent and self-sufficient, and does not require any superior power to govern it. Jains also refrain from marrying outside the religion, which has accelerated their decline. The Jain symbol is the reverse swastika from Sanskrit and is displayed in Hindu businesses and homes to signify good faith and prosperity. The vertical arms represent heaven at the top and hell below, with earth and the animal/plant kingdom horizontally across the centre.

Our first stop is at Karkala Temple to see the statue of Lord Bahubali or the 'one with strong shoulders'. He was a local priest who fought his brother Bharat and won his kingdom, but having done so gave it all up for meditation and prayer for 12 years. Behind the great statue are statues of the 24 naked *tirthankara*. The statue of Lord Bahubali was voted by Indians the first of the Seven Wonders of India.

From the hilltop we look across palm-covered countryside to another hill about a kilometre away. On top is the Chaturmukha or the Four Faced Jain Temple. A frangipani tree is in flower beside the steps going down. A hamlet of brown-tiled single-storey houses is hidden under the coconut palms. A modern two-storey white mansion has recently been built. This is India at its best.

Our final stop is in the holy Jain City of Moodabidri to visit the 15th-century Thousand Pillar Temple. Even if the count was a bit out, it is some fantastic place. Every pillar has been sculptured with a different design. Inside the locked central shrine is the 8-foot idol of Chandranah. In a corner at the back of the temple is the shrine to Humanan, the Monkey God or Superman. Wow again!

It is time to close the circle. Andrew and I visited the Ajanta and Ellora Caves as well as the Khajaraho Temple with its Kama sutra sculptures. I have now learnt that the cave temple in Ellora in Maharasta near Bombay is Jain. 'Andrew, let's do the trip again but by chauffeur driven limo with a guide like David to tell us all.'

On April 6th we come back to Bombay, which is now Mumbai. Not far from the quay we see a vast number of Volkswagens lined up. For input or export, I ask our guide Suba. 'For export,' she replies. She welcomes us to her 'City of Contrasts', the most cosmopolitan city in India with 22 million inhabitants and, with a vast and growing industrial hinterland, the driving force in the financial and commercial future of the country. India, however, is different to the East Asian economies, which are dependent on a manufacturing base, which has required huge capital investment. India is a world high-tech power whose strength is based on its brains rather than its brawn, which does not require high capital investment. Everywhere we have been, from city to country village, we have seen shops advertising: 'Learn programming here'. With English very widely spoken, I can see a great future for India, particularly if it devolves its solution-solving skills to the smaller cities in the different states. If the country gets high-speed broadband and the Indian diaspora remains loyal to its roots, I put my money on India.

We stop at the security barrier at the exit to the harbour and a smart young man in fatigues gets on the coach. Normally this is a formality and we just wave our documents in the air, but we are in India. He checks every 'Landing Permission Card' against a photocopy of our passports and then checks we look like our photo. The British instructed the Indians well in bureaucracy; but it is even worse in the UK. Sadly bureaucracy can stifle a country's progress. However, the warmth of welcome is immediately apparent, everyone waves.

Our first photo-op is outside the Victoria Terminus railway station, built in 1888 in Italian Gothic style similar to St. Pancras Station. There used to be a statue of Queen Victoria in the station forecourt but the rain eroded it and it fell down!

Next to the coach stop is a cannon, behind which is a plaque to two soldiers who gave their lives on 15th October 1857, when the British Army brutally subjected them to cannonball fire. 'Their martyrdom inspired millions of Indians to fight for their country's independence. We salute them and all other freedom fighters of India's struggle for their independence.' This was at the start of the 'Indian Mutiny' as the British call it and 'The First War of Independence' according to the Indians.

HITCHHIKING TO INDIA IN 1962

Marine Drive is the main promenading, jogging and meditating place in the city. At night, lights along the seafront give the Drive its nickname of the Queen's Necklace. At the far end is a Senior Citizens garden to seaward with fat pigeons being fed. Chowpatty Beach is a broad expanse of sand, but the water looks most unwelcoming, muddy, shallow and probably polluted.

We turn inland and wealthy property continues until we arrive at the 27-floor (with three floors for car parking), $2-billion pad of a Jain who made his money from textiles, then investing on the stock exchange and now into petrol and Bollywood. Like so many other rich Indians, the Jains are very generous to charitable organisations. To the right is a city centre golf course then an Aston Martin dealership. Cool!

The other side of life then hits us. A girl beggar is running beside the coach with a live chicken on her head. The word has got around that the tourists have arrived. We stop on a railway bridge and a swarm of hustling children arrive offering trinkets and postcards for 'a dollar'. Young and old men were selling peacock fans, bags and other goods for high prices, which rapidly descended as we moved on to our next attraction, the Dhobi Ghat, where ten thousand men were working in an open-air laundry. Suba, our guide, offers the ladies of our party some advice: 'Now, sisters, let some of the men do the housework'. Clothes are first boiled then pummelled and beaten until clean. Finally they are rinsed and hung out to dry in the sun. This process is highly energy efficient. Items are brought from hotels and homes by bicycle or handcart and are never lost as the workers use a coding system to identify every piece of laundry. Clever Indians!

On the bridge is a man with his tame cow feeding on some hay. Extraordinary! Beside the roads are five-storey tenements with wooden balconies originally built by the

Portuguese for the cotton mill workers. A high export tax was imposed by the British to safeguard Lancashire industry. The buildings are now threatened with demolition, as land in central Mumbai is fearfully expensive. Skyscrapers are beginning to rise up.

The high point of my return to India is next on our agenda: Mani Bhavan at 19 Laburnum Road, the three-storey house that Mahatma Gandhi worked in for much of the time he was in India. His absolute belief in truth and non-violence led India to their independence in 1947. Over the years the driving force against British Imperialism, he has become the undisputed hero of his country. Fifty years after our visit, India has changed the political winners but at least India has a democracy.

In my search for religions on our Asian trip I am surprised and rather taken by our next stop. The Krishna Temple would win the popularity stakes if body count were the measure. It is packed with young people listening to a lecture. At least two days' study of my photos of the exhibits at the Temple would produce a document, but the following is my understanding of the Hare Krishna Movement. In 1965, His Divine Grace A. C. Bhaktivedanta Swami Prabhupada travelled from India to the US and began the International Society for Krishna Consciousness (ISKCON), which now has 500 temples, farm communities and schools, with a membership of 3 million in the West and fifty million worldwide. He passed away in 1977, but his disciples pass on his message.

Members of the Hare Krishna Movement follow India's ancient Vedic literature, which form the basis of the world's third largest religion, Hinduism. The Vedic literature establishes non-violence as the foundation of vegetarianism and a peaceful society. They believe in reincarnation. The Hare Krishna chant is a spiritual sound vibration that purifies the consciousness and awakens love for God.

A few hundred followers are seated on the floor listening

to an unmarried monk wearing a saffron dhoti. Time does not allow us to join the congregation, who are a happy bunch giving us a welcoming smile. I have just one question. Why are the sexes segregated with rows for men at the front and women at the back? The temple houses 140 monks and provides meals for a larger number. I wander off in search of literature and Jannie suspects I am signing up.

Krishna, the blue God, manifests before us a multifarious personality. He is a delightful child, slayer of fiery demons, lord of abundance, protector of cows and natural wealth, a romantic lover, a hero, statesman and exponent of India's greatest philosophical doctrine, the Bhagavata Gita. The tale of Krishna is over 2,500 years old and has inspired poets, painters and artists.

The Malabar Hills stretch out to sea at the north end of the great Back Bay. The finest houses and best view are here. Our destination is the Hanging Gardens, which have been built on top of the cover of the city's reservoir. The cover was added because Parsees left their corpses in the neighbouring area, to be eaten clean by vultures in the Towers of Silence. Vultures are messy feeders and would drop chunks of meat into the reservoir, to the detriment of its drinking quality. So a cover was constructed above which is a beautiful garden for relaxing and walking.

Parsees worship the elements of nature: water, sky, earth and fire, so cremation is never allowed. Mumbai's Authority, however, objected to the presence of vultures in the city, so the Parsees have come up with a brilliant 21st-century solution to body disposal. Solar panels and chemicals are used to convert the flesh into powder. Unfortunately the ghoulish process is hidden from public view by a high wall. I manage to scale it and look over and see . . . you've guessed it, photovoltaic panels.

An Arabic couple was amused by my antics and started a conversation; their English was excellent. He wore a dish-dash and she the full works. They were obviously very much in love as she cuddled up to him when he asked me to take a photo. I have now two Yemeni friends.

The Parsees are a diminishing group, numbering 80,000 worldwide with 60,000 in India of which 40,000 are in Mumbai. Parsees cannot convert from other religions and must be born of two Parsee parents. They obviously hope their own children marry other Parsees. Also known as Zoroastrians, they originally came from Persia. On the whole they are wealthy with the most well known follower being Tata, the owner of Jaguar Land Rover and vast industries in India. 60% of Tata's profit goes to charities related to education and medicine. Indians suffering from cancer can be treated for free at the Tata Cancer Hospital.

Our penultimate stop is the Prince of Wales Museum, which was founded in 1922, though the building was started in 1905 to celebrate the future George V's visit. It became a hospital during WWI. It is a fine example of the Indo-Saracenic, or 16th-century Muslim, style. The garden outside is a gem, watered by 'Rainwater Harvesting'. An egret watches us queue in two columns, one for males and one for females. How can a four-and-a-half-hour tour take in everything we have seen so far plus one of the finest collections of art, archaeology and natural history in the country, when we have just 20 minutes for our visit?

We choose to visit Tibet through the eyes of the photographer Li Gotami in 1947–49. Tibetans have imbibed Buddhist precepts of compassion and friendship. This has contributed to the gentleness, warmth and unreserved friendliness they show in the midst of their otherwise seemingly hostile world. Here are some of the subjects on display: their mantra; incense burning; miniature stupas; water, tea and beer pots; musical instruments including cymbals, trumpets and drums; the royal dynasty of Tibet; Buddhism; Lamaism; deities; saints; siddhas; monasteries;

thousand armed and thousand headed Avalokitesvara; shrines; religion and votive clay tablets.

In conclusion the Museum has a wealth of Tibetan objects. Compare this with the story our Shanghai guide had told us just a month earlier. Visiting Hong Kong she bought some books on Tibet. Back at home they were confiscated. Also consider the Beijing guide who had her TV satellite dish confiscated, as people should use the apartment block's shared and censured hub. My argument in favour of India's quality of life is very strong.

The great challenge is to modify the exodus from the countryside to ever-greater cities. Our waiter comes from the 'small' town near Mangalore where the Jain Thousand Pillar Temple is situated; he went to a school next door. His town, with a million inhabitants, has four engineering colleges. Yet the young flock to cities where foreign companies provide jobs. He agrees that if there were investment in local graduate employment, the exodus to the cities would be greatly slowed down.

A final factor in measuring the quality of life is shopping. India is almost devoid of supermarkets: local shopping provides fresh food instead. India has a remarkable challenge ahead, and I just hope it can see there is more to life than just material advancement.

Our final stop is a pilgrimage to the Gateway to India, near to the place where Andrew and I left on our way home on the deck of *MS Dumra* up the Persian Gulf. The 26-metre-high Gateway to India is a symbol of nearly 200 years of British imperialism. It was built to commemorate the arrival of King George V and Queen Mary in 1911. Construction was completed in 1924. It was here that the British troops paraded before sailing for home on August 17th 1947, just two days after Independence Day.

Interestingly, unlike in 1962, hustlers and beggars are missing. Now we leave a country in the throes of a General

Election. As well as bureaucracy, railways and cricket, the British left behind a democracy. One day perhaps we will come back.

When we discuss our trip of a lifetime there are two questions that I ask people.

The first is the easier. China and India could well be the countries of the future. To me, one was a free-range chicken and the other was a battery hen.

China is the battery hen. The battery hen is highly productive but it has no freedom.

India on the other hand offers great freedom so it is my free-range chicken. A free-range chicken has a choice: it can wander off and be eaten by a fox or it can return to its coop at night. A battery hen has no choice.

Along Marine Dive we come to the most remarkable sight on my Asian tour. It confirms why India is far ahead of China in my Quality of Life Index. I am not being facetious by saying this alone differentiates the battery chickens and the free-range chickens. At least a thousand people are playing cricket in a mile-long park. First class matches are sharing the ground with perhaps 50 knock-about games. It is an example of the wonderful chaos of the country. Hackney Marsh in the early 1960s was much the same with numerous football games being played on 100 pitches.

When we left England in early January 2104, I wanted to find a country, which has more than one religion and more than one ethnic group, but which lives in harmony. This is the second question. Which country was this?

Sadly India cannot be the answer here, because even today race riots occur. In December 1992 after a rally turned violent, a large crowd of Hindu volunteers, many from the World Hindu Council and also the Bharatiya Janata Party, destroyed the 16th-century Babr Masjid Mosque in Ayodhya, Uttar Pradesh, which they claimed stood on the birth site of Rama. Several months of rioting between the Hindu and Muslim communities in many parts of India, including attacks by the police on Muslims in Mumbai, resulted in 2,000 deaths. The right wing nationalist BJP, one of whose controversial policies is the building of a Ram temple in Ayodhya, and the Congress Party are India's two largest parties. To India's credit, and this could make my judgment on the question suspect, after the riots the communities of different religions didn't turn on each other, but lived together.

The answer to my second question is Malaysia. On the mainland we made visits to Malacca, Kuala Lumpur, fabulous Penang and Langkawi on the border with Thailand. On Borneo, we stopped off in Kuching in Sarawak and Koto Kinabalu in Sabah. Our guides were Muslim Malay, Buddhist Chinese, Hindu Indian and a Roman Catholic from an ex-head-hunting tribe called the Iban. 'What was the magic ingredient that made for harmony between the religions and races?' I asked. 'Respect', they all answered. In Sarawak our indigenous Iban guide put it perfectly: 'We live and let live; our difference becomes our unifying force'.

In 1962 and today, there has too often been too little respect for the other religions. But there was something else, which was immensely important. Before the British granted Malaysia its independence, they insisted that the different religious-based parties should form a united party, which has lasted ever since. I contrast this stroke of genius with India, where the British in 1929 decided that political parties should be faith-based. This led to the massacres at the time of partition. Later, after his mother's assassination, Rajiv Gandhi chose quiet diplomacy rather arms to solve the Sikh-Hindu conflict. Is this another lesson we should learn?

The partition of 1947 left wounds that still refuse to heal. Today, according to Google Maps, the 30 miles from Lahore to Amritsar can be walked in 10 hours or driven in 110 hours via Islamabad, Kashmir, Xinjiang, Tibet, Nepal

INDIA FIFTY YEARS ON

and Chandigarh. Such is the historic hatred between the two countries that this is the recommended route to cross where the Punjab state was divided in 1947. Pakistan, a tragedy now compared to 1962, still sees the imaginary influence of India in the overflow from the wars in Afghanistan.

In contrast, India is a genuine financial and industrial powerhouse, but sadly the rich – and these can be incredibly rich – and the poor are planets apart.

CHAPTER 17
THE BALKANS IN 2015, REFUGEES AND SYRIA

Online help

There's a young refugee knocking at the door
And I clicked on a button that said let him in
There's a young refugee knocking at the door
And I clicked on a button that said send him food
There's a young refugee knocking at our door
Our door?
Are you sure?
And just one?
Or is it more?
There's a young refugee knocking on my door
My door?
Are you sure?
But I supported the petition and sent the money
My door?
Are you sure?

Andrew Macalpine 2015

At the end of October 2015 Jannie and I go to exquisite Venice on a trip through the Balkans to check out how they have changed since 1962 and to witness potentially the greatest migration in the century so far. We are warned 'not to buy goods from street sellers as this is considered a crime'. African migrants have sold their bangles and CDs for years. Now they are criminals. Is this a foretaste of the future for those arriving in Europe today?

THE BALKANS IN 2015, REFUGEES AND SYRIA

Is the smuggler who shipped him from Africa also a criminal? He will benefit financially, so the answer is yes. What do we say about Angela Merkel, who has invited 800,000 Syrian migrants to come to her country and will benefit from the doctors and engineers that will help Germany and all the others who in the long run will pay for German pensions? Before we cross over to Slovenia, I would like an answer to this question.

Since 1966, we had always driven from England to Greece or Denmark through Germany and we liked Germany and the Germans. We are almost part of the Klingler family in the guesthouse Goldener Greifen in one of Europe's most beautiful small towns, Rothenburg ob der Tauber. On our return from the Balkans, on 1st November, I pointed out to Frau Klingler that some in the Balkans had suggested Angela Merkel had made a mistake and that she had also been guilty of lack of planning. She replied that it was not a mistake and that Angela Merkel's decision was based on economic factors.

'We need people who will come to work as we have work for them', she said. 'We are a Christian country but they must follow our rules such as the respect we have for women's rights.' She agreed that it was a repeat of the 1950s *Gastarbeiter* policy. I then mentioned Syria. She was worried about Putin. 'We have a number of Russian guests and they are good people.'

It is 25th October 2015. We are by beautiful Lake Bled on the road to the border of Slovenia and Austria. The view is stunning, from the castle towards the snow-topped Julian Alps to the north and the shimmering water far below as the evening sun turns the lake into a silver sheet with the little island in the centre. Is this heaven? I asked the same question in Anatolia as I looked down on the crystal clear sparkling river below. My answer now is the same as it was in 1962, when there were underlying issues that were disturbing –

then it was the migration of the Armenians. Today it is the migration of the Syrians, Afghans and others. 1001 years ago, Bled Castle was built by migrant Slavic tribes from the north. Perhaps in a hundred years time the migrant Muslim tribes of the East will have been assimilated.

We have just visited Ljubljana, named after the Slav word for love. This magical little capital squashed between Castle Hill and the Ljubljanica River will one day become the next Prague. Is there love now? On the surface of course there is. Here I ask our hostess Nina if she is afraid – of the refugees. She is worried about the future as there is uncertainty but not afraid as the mass of migrants are not coming through Ljubljana but passing through to Austria and Germany via Maribor, exactly the route Andrew and I took 53 years before. (Within a week the Austrians were threatening to close the Maribor border.)

In 1962 we had travelled through what was the Socialist Republic of Slovenia within the Federal Socialist Republic of Yugoslavia. It has now its independence. It is a member of the European Union, uses the euro and has signed the Schengen Agreement, which ended border controls and demolished the barriers to free movement in Europe with many of the customs buildings disappearing. Nina says that you drive through into Italy and not notice you are entering another country. Today we are at the frontier of a mass migration, and border controls are back in place. Tomorrow we could see the European Union start to break up.

We move on to Split in Croatia. What better recommendation for a city than the Roman Emperor Diocletian, who chose this beautiful bay to build his retirement home in 295AD. And what a home it was, and still is, as the immense walls of the palace still stand. At its centre is the octagonal mausoleum where he was buried, which was converted to an exquisite church. In his long life as emperor he killed a huge number of Christians. On

THE BALKANS IN 2015, REFUGEES AND SYRIA

retirement he was succeeded by Constantine who moved the centre of the Empire to Constantinople, now Istanbul, made Christianity the official religion and precipitated the division of the Holy Roman Empire into Eastern Orthodox and Western Catholic based in Rome. What irony! 1,600 years later in 1942 the Catholic Croat *Ustaše* slaughtered the Orthodox Serbs. And in August 1995, 150,000 Serbs were forcibly expelled from Knin in the district of Krajina in Croatia, inland from Split. This was, at the time, the biggest mass exodus in Europe since the expulsion of Sudetan Germans from Czechoslovakia in 1945.

In Split, our host Ivitsa, little Ivan or John, or Johnny as he likes to be called, confirmed my theory that, in 1962, the students in the Croatian capital of Zagreb would have refused to talk politics as everyone was afraid of talking to their neighbour, as the Serb-dominated secret service, whom he described as like the *Stasi* in Eastern Germany, had spies everywhere.

Ivitsa believed that Angela Merkel had made a major mistake as far as Europe was concerned when in June she personally made an open-ended commitment to invite the Syrian refugees to Germany. He said that her claim that '*Wir schaffen das*' ('We will cope') was short lived. She waived Germany's right to return Syrian asylum-seekers to their European country of entry, suspended the Dublin II accord, the objective of which is to identify as quickly as possible the Member State responsible for examining an asylum application, and to prevent abuse of asylum procedures. She then decided to do away with all effective vetting of asylum applications submitted by Syrians. This encouraged more refugees to come, so by August she was trying to impose a one-off plan to redistribute 120,000 asylum-seekers across the EU, despite bitter opposition from Hungary, Slovakia and the Czechs. He was worried that this would split a united Europe.

In October Merkel was in Turkey, personally requesting

them to keep the refugees with promises of billions of euros and a quick entrance into the European Union. Ivitsa compared this with the ten years Croatia had to wait to earn entrance, and also to the hasty decision that allowed Greece to enter the EEC, the result of which we are now suffering from.

Ivitsa considered that the decision by Angela Merkel might not have been a mistake for Germany, as it would get new workers. If, however, Germany is forced to close its border against the refugees the mistake will become a catastrophe for Croatia and the other Balkan countries, as they will not be able to cope.

Croatia's original enthusiasm for the European Union has since waned. Its economy has been static with the first signs of growth coming in 2015. It will be a further 4-5 years before it joins the Eurozone.

Within ten years of Tito's death in 1980, the two major republics, Croatia and Serbia, under their powerful leaders Franjo Tudjman and Slobodan Milošević realised that by splitting Bosnia they could achieve their own nations. Like all turf wars, the gang leaders fell out over the spoils. Croats shelled Serb eastern Mostar and the famous bridge over the Neretva to destruction, and Serbs under their local strong men Karadic and Mladic, from the heights above the city, tried to bomb Sarajevo to extinction.

In early summer 1995, Robert Frasure, the assistant on the ground to Richard Holbrooke, the US Secretary of State for European and Canadian Affairs, struck a deal between Milošević, Tudjman and Izetbegović, the Bosnian leader to end the sanctions and hence the war. Washington turned it down and fighting started again, with the Bosnian Serbs then carrying out a policy of ethic cleansing including the cold-blooded murder of 8,000 unarmed Muslims men in Srebrenica in retaliation for the expulsion of the Serbs from Croatian Krajina. The latter was supported by President

Clinton, who, with re-election coming up, reversed his decision over the Frasure Plan in August, which eventually led to the end of the Bosnian War.

Carl Bildt, the European Union mediator in the former Yugoslavia, called for the International Tribunal on War Crimes in the Hague to investigate President Tudjman for shelling Knin. Bildt asked: 'If we accept that it is alright for Tudjman to cleanse Croatia of its Serbs, then how on earth can we object if one day Milošević sends his army in to clean out the Albanians from Kosovo?' Bildt was a prophet as this is exactly what Milošević did four years later. After three months he succumbed to massive bombing of Serbia so ending the war in Yugoslavia, 85 years after Austro-Hungary's shelling of Belgrade started the First World War. The lesson learnt by the West was a false one. Bombing Afghanistan, Iraq and now Syria has led to destabilisation of each country and huge refugee flows.

Our next stop was Dubrovnik, a gem at the southern end of Croatia. Discussing the civil war, our hostess, Dejaira philosophically declared that, 'ordinary people got on but the problem was the politicians'.

A highlight of this walled city, which stands on a rocky outcrop into the Adriatic Sea is the Rector's Palace. When Dubrovnik was an independent state, the rector was elected to run the state for just a one-month term. He would leave his family at home and move into the Palace. By having only a short time in power, corruption was eliminated. Time moves on: the current election in Croatia is between the only two parties – the one in power is less than efficient; the opposition is led by a man on corruption charges!

We discussed the issue of the Serbian and Croatian languages, as I was still fluent with my four words of Serbo-Croat. 'They are effectively the same,' claimed Dejaira, so rubbishing Croat dictator Franjo Tudjman's claim that the Croats had lost their language.

On 1st October 1991, shells rained down on Dubrovnik from the self-declared independent Bosnian Serb Republic behind the mountains to the north east of the city. Dejaira's mother gathered up the children and they ran, not knowing where they would finish up. Other women did the same. Only the men remained to defend their homes. She compared this with the refugees from Syria, who seem to be predominantly men and who leave their families to face the bombs. 'People never learn', Dejaira declared.

Our final port on our Balkan reunion was Kotor in Montenegro, which uses the euro but is not yet a member of the EU. It will join NATO in 2016. Once again as tourists we did not realise the recent history. We drove up a single-lane road with 24 hairpin bends. At 900 metres we viewed the longest fjord in southern Europe way below us and then crossed over the mountains to pass through the Njegusi valley with deciduous trees in every possible shade of orange, gold, red and yellow to finish at the old royal capital of Cetinje where, at the end of the 19th century, King Nicholas, the last of the 200-year-old Petrovic dynasty, had three sons and nine daughters, whom he married off to other European royal houses.

Our new hostess, Anna was full of jokes: the gypsy house with car wrecks in the front yard was the eco-centre; the Bosnians were so stupid and the Montenegrins were so lazy that they never finished the 100 metre race, as the Bosnian got lost and the Montenegrin lay down to rest. For the first time on our Balkan adventure we heard the ethnic undertones that are rooted in its history.

Her statistics were interesting. The population of Montenegro was 76% Orthodox, 15% Muslim and 9% Catholic. There were many inter-religion marriages. 'Everyone is treated equally. When the Orthodox build a church, the Muslims build a mosque as well.' The country had kept out of the Croatian and Bosnian wars in the 1990s, though sanctions had destroyed much of the industry, and factories closed. I told Anna that we were in Corfu in 1999 when the planes flew north at great height above our peaceful island.

'Ah yes', she said. 'The NATO aircraft were on their way to bomb Montenegro. I was a teenager then.' The plan was to smash the federal armament dumps in the country. From the height they were flying their accuracy could not be guaranteed and there was 'collateral damage'. This was another name for civilian casualties. The war in neighbouring Kosovo had been triggered off by Milošević's policy of ethnic cleansing of Albanians, which she denied, though she knew about the Albanians' ethnic cleansing of the Serbs.

Misha Glenny in his wonderful book *The Balkans 1804–1999* wrote: 'The propaganda war accompanying the conflict in Kosovo was intense even by modern standards'. From Anna's reaction Milošević won it. NATO would justify its first war outside its treaty area on humanitarian grounds. Milošević would say the West was behaving like Hitler in attacking a sovereign nation and bombing Belgrade.

The initial result was a massive movement of refugees out of Kosovo. 'The same is happening from Syria now. Today's news said that the refugees are being robbed by Albanians in Macedonia', claimed Anna. I hope she was wrong, as robbing refugees we have learnt from history, particularly Armenian refugees, is a very serious crime.

* * * * *

So what is the solution to the refugee crisis, which could well destroy the European Union? Surely we should be looking at the source of the problem. There is no coincidence that so many refugees come from Afghanistan, Iraq and Syria, where war still drives out the young men, for economic reasons or to avoid call-up. In these countries bombs rain down and towns are destroyed.

Interestingly, there are almost no refugees from Iran, where the Islamic Republic offers a future for their young. Iran is the one country where I believe change has been positive since 1962. With Obama's initiatives to bring the Islamic Republic in from the cold by quiet diplomacy, is it too optimistic to think that there is recognition that the CIA coup was wrong and that American hegemony, perhaps driven by Cold War paranoia, might be coming to an end?

Even the future of Turkey is not certain. The mythical glorification of Turkish ethnic identity, espoused by the young man in Istanbul in 1962, is alive today in Turkey's third largest party, though at long last the Kurds are represented in the Turkish Parliament. Is Turkey's opposition to ISIS as strong as its opposition to the Kurds? Can they ever get autonomy?

Angela Merkel's offer of EU membership to Turkey is a high price to pay for the maintenance of the refugee camps. We should remember when a weak Greece was offered membership. So what is the solution to the refugee crisis?

Let me return to the second question in the chapter on India. Which multi-religious country is in harmony? Our 1962 trip did not produce one. The vicar in Corfu replied to this question: 'It used to be Syria'. I checked this out with others who knew the Middle East and they agreed.

Therefore one should ask: why is there none now, whilst there was harmony ten years ago?

Today the base of the Islamic State is beside the Euphrates River between Ar Raqqah and Deir ez-Zur, where the Armenians were finally massacred over a hundred years ago. The Sunni fundamentalists of ISIS, under the leadership of the new Caliph, Abu Bakr al Baghdadi, see their fight as an existential battle against the Alawite Shia Assad and the Christians, which had been forecast in one of the sayings of the Prophet that the final showdown would fought in a location called Dabiq, a small town in Northern Syria.

THE BALKANS IN 2015, REFUGEES AND SYRIA

Dabiq is now the symbolic destination of jihadis from around the world. It is also the title of their monthly online magazine.

In 2007, Syria had a so-called presidential election. Observers suggested that even the opposition agreed that, though the confirmation vote for Bashar al-Assad to stay on for a second term was 97%, he would still have received a majority in a free vote, as he had support across all faiths in a secular state, he was a reformer, things were getting better and Syria was safer than neighbouring countries. There was, however, corruption and the brutal security service inherited in 2000 from his father Hafez al-Assad.

Charles R Lister in *The Syrian Jihad* says Bashar al-Assad, on taking power, 'presided over a partial revival of Sunni Islam within state-accepted circles and set about establishing friendly and eventually rather cosy relationships with moderate Sunni leaders, who were duly installed in positions of authority. Bashar appointed Sunnis into the positions of foreign minister (2006), vice-president (2006), deputy minister for economic affairs (2005) and ambassador to London (2004). At the start of 2011, despite the still dominant role of Alawites and the Assad family within Syria's governing elite, the country was largely stable along its very varied ethnic and sectarian lines. Bashar al-Assad had in fact fostered a partial integration into officialdom of not only Sunnis, but also members of Syria's Christian, Druze and Kurdish communities.'

According to Eugene Rogan's *The Arabs: A History* in 2011, Syria was almost the last Arab country to be affected by the Arab Spring: Assad did enjoy a degree of legitimacy and public support that made him different to other Arab autocrats. He was hostile towards Israel and pro-Hamas and Hezbollah, which was popular amongst Syrians but not so in the West. In February he drove himself to the Umayyad Mosque to take part in prayers to mark the Prophet

Muhammad's birthday and he strolled through souks with a low-security profile.

Though unemployment was high as elsewhere in the Middle East, the youth had little to complain about. A typical comment was: 'There is a lot of government help for the youth. They give us free books, free schools, free universities. Why should there be a revolution?' The initial 'Facebook' demonstrators in Damascus were outnumbered by the security forces.

However, on 18th March 2011, fifteen teenagers in the farming town of Deraa, on the Syrian-Jordanian border, painted slogans on walls and were arrested and tortured; demonstrations followed. Assad immediately dispatched a high-level delegation to Deraa in a vain attempt to diffuse the tense situation. The government's men cashiered the governor, promised to bring those responsible for firing on the demonstrators to justice, and released the fifteen young detainees.

From the outset of the Syrian uprising, the vast majority of the army remained loyal to the regime and proved its willingness to fire on its fellow citizens. In July 2011, a group of military defectors formed the Free Syrian Army, and in August, five days after President Obama had called for Assad to step down, a group of civilian exiles created the Syrian National Council in Istanbul. It squabbled amongst itself without offering a realistic alternative to the Assad regime.

According to *The Foreign Policies of Middle East States* by Raymond Hinnebusch and Anoushirivan Ehteshami, Erdogan's AKP 'opportunistically identified Syria as a chance to profit by extending its influence closer to home'. The day before Obama's call for Assad to step down, Turkey's foreign minister went to Damascus and made a similar request. Just under a month later Turkey cut all formal contacts with the Syrian regime and gave notice that a

THE BALKANS IN 2015, REFUGEES AND SYRIA

strong, bilateral sanctions package was in preparation.

In November, Qatar and Saudi Arabia took the initiative in prompting the Arab League to isolate Syria and dry up the regime's access to economic resources.

Qatar, home to the America's largest re-positioning bases outside the USA, spent over $3 billion in arming anti-Assad fighters and in prompting allies in the West and in the Arab world to do more to hasten the collapse of the Assad regime.

On 22nd February 2012 at the UN, Vitaly Churkin, Russia's Permanent Representative since 2006, proposed that Syria's president, Bashar al-Assad, could step down as part of a peace deal. He said the West:
1. should not give arms to the opposition,
2. should get a dialogue going between the opposition and Assad straight away, and
3. should find an elegant way for Assad to step aside.

Nothing happened because the West were convinced that Assad would be thrown out of office in a few weeks so there was no need to do anything.

In 2013 the Chief of the Defence Staff, General Sir David Richards, asked Cameron if he was certain we were backing the right side as he felt there was a case for letting Assad win, because at least that would put the population out of their misery.

On a visit to London in June 2014, the veteran diplomat Henry Kissinger pleaded with his audience to see Russia as an ally, not an enemy, against Muslim fundamentalism.

Perhaps the West should put aside their distrust of the Russians and work together with them and Assad plus hopefully the non-fundamental opposition against the real menace of today, the religious fanatics.

Or do we want to be involved in the next battle in the not so Cold War between Sunni, supported by Saudi Arabia that demands Assad should go, and Shia? Patrick Cockburn in *The Rise of Islamic State* says: 'In Syria, the Americans backed a plan by Saudi Arabia to build up a "Southern Front" based in Jordan that would be hostile to the Assad Government and al-Qaeda-type rebels in the north and east. The powerful but supposedly moderate Yarmouk Brigade, reportedly the planned recipient of anti-aircraft missiles from Saudi Arabia, was intended to be the leading element in this new formation. But numerous videos show that the Yarmouk Brigade has frequently fought in collaboration with JAN, the official Al-Qaeda affiliate. Since it was likely that, in the midst of battle, these two groups would share their munitions, Washington was effectively allowing advanced weaponry to be handed over to its deadliest enemy.'

Let Assad, a Syrian not some puppet imposed by the West, defeat the Islamic State so that peace might be brought to Syria, the refugees can return home and, with enough financial support, the country can rebuild itself.

Already half the population are refugees, that is 12 million, the same number displaced in India, and 250,000 have been killed.

In 2012, Kofi Annan, on behalf of the UN, proposed a political compromise but the West insisted on Assad resigning, so Annan resigned instead. In January 2014 Lakhdar Brahimi, backed by the UN and the Arab League, chaired a conference in Geneva but the US Secretary of State declared on the first day, Assad must go.

Let a third attempt of diplomacy be more successful. The time has come for serious talking between the US, Russia, Turkey and Iran behind closed doors at the UN.

CHAPTER 18
THREE DAYS THAT SAVED THE EURO

'The ruthlessness that her finance minister, Wolfgang Schäuble, displayed in bouncing Greece into total capitulation at the July summit, has done lasting damage to Germany's reputation for giving Europe a lead that can transcend petty national rivalries.'

Guardian July 2015

We had arrived in Lubeck, Germany on Sunday 12th July in ignorance of what was happening in Brussels. That weekend would decide the future of Greece in Europe and possible of the European Union itself. In a very long article in the *Guardian* on 22nd October, Ian Traynor summarised these dramatic events, which would finish in not only a European compromise but also seriously damage Germany's reputation for giving Europe a lead. The following is a shortened version of Ian Traynor's article.

Late on the afternoon of Friday 10th July, as European finance ministers were packing their bags for Brussels to attend yet another meeting on the Greek debt crisis, a shocking email from Berlin landed in the inboxes of a very small number of top officials. Earlier that week, the Greek prime minister, Alexis Tsipras, had been given an ultimatum by his fellow European leaders: deliver a radical new blueprint for economic reform and spending cuts – or face bankruptcy.

Tsipras had delivered a new set of proposals, but before officials could meet in Brussels to discuss them, the German finance minister, Wolfgang Schäuble, delivered a pre-emptive strike: if the Greek government would not undertake more drastic reforms, the German email said, 'Greece should be offered swift negotiations on a time-out from the Eurozone'.

'It was clear', one recipient said. 'It was written down. It was harsh. It was brutal.' Schäuble, the most experienced politician in power in Europe, had gone for the jugular – and the email sent alarm bells ringing in Paris, Rome, Frankfurt and Brussels.

'It was never officially distributed – only to core people', said a senior official involved in the meetings, who saw the email on the Friday evening.

Schäuble's proposal popped up on screens in the upper reaches of the European Commission at around 6pm that Friday. It took the form of a one-page memo – what Eurocrats call a 'non-paper' – sent by Thomas Steffen, one of Schäuble's deputies in the German finance ministry. As well as calling for Greece's suspension from the single currency for at least five years, it also proposed that Athens should transfer assets worth €50bn – a quarter of the national wealth – into a trust fund located in Luxembourg and controlled by the European Stability Mechanism, the Eurozone's bailout fund. It would be a massive asset-stripping enterprise, modelled on West Germany's privatisation of East German state property after the fall of the Berlin Wall in 1989: gradually, the assets would be sold off, and the proceeds used to pay off Greek debt.

'A lot of people were really scandalised', a senior diplomat in Brussels said. 'It was incredible. No country could have accepted this.' For Matteo Renzi, the Italian prime minister, the Schäuble ultimatum was an untenable exercise in German humiliation of Greece. It had to be stopped.

There were those among the leaders, central bankers, and 19 eurozone finance ministers who wondered whether Schäuble was serious. But senior figures at the European Central Bank, the European Commission and the Luxembourg-based euro bailout fund, who had been involved in negotiations all along, realised he was not bluffing – in fact, they had known about Schäuble's plans for a long time. They believe that Schäuble made his mind up at the beginning of the year – even before Tsipras was elected as prime minister – that the Eurozone had to be protected from weaklings: Greece was a liability and had to go.

At the age of 73, Schäuble exudes authority and gravitas. The Christian Democrat, who uses a wheelchair after an assassination attempt in 1990 left him paralysed from the waist down, is the longest-serving MP in postwar Germany, and has been at the heart of government since 1989. He ran the negotiations over German reunification, and he was there at the birth of the euro at Maastricht in 1992.

Schäuble's manoeuvre on Friday 10th July was breathtaking because it broke a taboo: membership of the euro is supposed to be irrevocable, and Schäuble demonstrated for the first time that Germany believed that the single currency was not forever – and that it was willing to push another country out. The revelation scared politicians across Europe. Someone like Renzi, reading of the proposed defenestration of Tsipras, could be forgiven for thinking: 'Am I next?'

Amid the endless arguments about what to do about Greece's unsustainable debt levels, the Schäuble paper stated baldly that under the rules governing the euro, there could be no debt 'haircut'. If Greece 'temporarily' left the euro, however, there could be much more generous action to reduce Greek debt. It sounded almost like bribery: 'We'll pay you to leave'.

Jean-Claude Juncker, the president of the European Commission, called President François Hollande in Paris: both men were determined to keep Greece in the euro, but they worried that if Merkel shared Schäuble's resolve to eject the Greeks, they would be powerless to stop her.

The three days that followed Schäuble's shock announcement would see finance ministers and central bankers locked in negotiations until midnight on Saturday before giving up in failure. They resumed their discussions on Sunday morning, before passing the baton to the national leaders – whose summit began at 4pm and ran through the night for 17 hours.

Kicking out the Greeks would have sent a terrifying signal to the weaker countries of the Eurozone, a warning that they must observe German-led instructions on sound budgets, austerity, public expenditure cuts, structural reforms. In short, if they did not become more German, they might become the new Greece.

In the end, it would come down to an unexpected last-minute compromise between Merkel and Tsipras, after 10 gruelling hours of overnight negotiations.

Tsipras had drastically changed his position on the terms of the bail out. Just days after the Greek people had rejected Europe's austerity terms, Tsipras performed a u-turn. In order to secure a third bail out, he produced a new set of tough reform proposals very similar to those he had just campaigned against. In a dramatic debate that ended in a vote several hours after midnight on the night of Friday 10th July, the Greek parliament gave Tsipras an overwhelming majority in support of his proposals. Unfortunately, these were the proposals that Schäuble had torn to shreds in his own memo – sent only a few hours before the Greek parliament sat down to vote.

It read: 'These proposals lack a number of paramount important reform areas to modernise the country. Labour market reform, reform of public sector, privatisation, banking sector, structural reforms are not sufficient. This is why these proposals cannot build the basis for a completely new, three-year programme.'

The officials from the European Commission and

the European Central Bank responded positively to the new Greek proposals: they gave the ministers an initial assessment of the Greek offer, which was viewed as Tsipras's first serious attempt at compromise, and a decent starting point for that weekend's negotiations.

The only one who directly challenged Schäuble on the fundamental point of ejecting Greece from the currency was Michel Sapin, his French counterpart. Publicly, Sapin would later dismiss the Schäuble paper as 'playing to the gallery'. Privately, he told the conference there was no legal provision for a country to leave the currency, temporarily or otherwise. Grexit was not an option. He was right, but this was a legalistic argument: Greece could not be formally ejected, but things could be made so difficult for Athens that it had no choice but to quit.

Schäuble did not say much, but after a few hours, he came up with another intervention calculated to shock. He proposed that all the Greek functionaries working in EU institutions should be ordered back home to Athens to rebuild their own country – on the grounds that they were precisely the kind of people the Greek state needed to overhaul its notoriously dysfunctional public administration. As protesting voices were raised, Schäuble, unrepentant, said: 'I'm the only one being creative here'.

At 4pm on Sunday 12th July, Merkel, Tsipras, and the other 17 Eurozone national leaders arrived for their summit meeting – along with the heads of the European Commision, the European Council, the European Central Bank and the IMF. The mood was already foul. The finance ministers' meeting the day before had failed to break the impasse, and the arriving politicians were tense and grim-faced.

Merkel and Tsipras spent more than 10 hours cloistered away from the summit, locked in their own psychodrama, which would make or break the euro. Tsipras could not accede to Schäuble's Luxembourg trust fund, which he saw as an outrageous European attempt to pilfer the Greek family silver.

By three in the morning, things looked bleak. The Greeks and the Germans were immovable. The French and the Italians were alarmed.

After half an hour of conversation, Hollande and Renzi resolved that Greece had to stay in the euro at all costs. Renzi then went to Merkel and Tsipras, and implored them to strike a deal. 'Angela', he told Merkel, 'now you have to decide'.

Almost everyone except Merkel and Tsipras regarded the final sticking point – the trust fund – as faintly ridiculous. The €50bn sum was seen by the others present as an irrelevance: nobody could imagine where Greece was going to find €50bn in assets to privatise, and the idea of surrendering them to a trust fund in Luxembourg was an insult to which no government could possibly agree.

In the end, Tsipras had capitulated to a script written in Berlin – reneging on his election pledges and splitting his own party, which did not prevent him from winning the snap election he called in September. But the bigger question may be what the chastening experience of that tense weekend did to Germany and Europe. Schäuble's bid to banish Greece from the eurozone had not succeeded, but it had resurrected the spectre of German bullying – the outcome of the summit, Munich's *Süddeutsche Zeitung* wrote, amounted to a demonstration of German power at the expense of German leadership.

* * * * *

I should now like to explain why Wolfgang Schäuble is wrong. These figures have been checked by an ex-actuary and very senior civil servant.

In 2011, Schäuble saw no contradiction between cutting the budget deficit and maintaining economic growth and said if you want to encourage more internal demand, you have to regain the confidence of the public by reducing deficits.

From 2008 to 2013, Greece's average deficit was over 11% of GDP. In 2014 it was 2.5% and so far in 2015 it has been 1.4%. For these two years the deficit in the UK has been 5.3% and 4.1%, in the US 5.8% and 4.6%, in France 3.8% and 3.1%. These OECD figures show that the Greeks are following Schäuble's rules but there is no internal demand and no public confidence.

The far greater issue is the lack of internal demand i.e. Gross Domestic Product. The Greek economy is not growing but shrinking. In the five years to 2014 the GDP dropped 26%, (the same as in the great US Depression). If the GDP had remained constant, Greece's Government Debt to GDP would be 130%, certainly too high, but better than Italy's and Portugal's. The current Government Debt is far too high at €240bn and can never be paid off from turning the deficit into a surplus.

A deficit is when tax received does not cover expenditure including interest paid on loans. For decades Greece's defence expenditure has been between twice and three times the European average, it has 1,300 tanks which is more than twice the number in the UK. Loans to buy German tanks, helicopters, submarines, etc. have partly created the impossible debt burden facing Greece today. Greece is Germany's biggest arms buyer. So why did Greece buy all this hardware? Ask the former defence minister who accepted a €8m bribe for paying €3bn for four faulty Class 214 submarines, which Greece didn't need. Ask Siemens that reached an out-of-court €300 million settlement over bribes paid during the 2004 Olympics.

So what does Schäuble suggest now? He has created a fund designated to cherrypick €50bn (£35bn) worth of Greek public assets and privatise them to pay the country's debts. He did this in 1990 with East German debt, which led to catastrophic psychological consequences and is still seen in the East as the policy of an occupying power. His idea of foreign countries controlling Greek assets and moving them abroad is an even more humiliating concept. The Greeks now see the Germans as the new bosses who pull the strings, want to own Greece's assets and control their future.

CHAPTER 19
LIFE IN A FINANCIAL GREEK TRAGEDY

These days the thousands that arrive daily in Corfu on their huge cruise ships and the tourists that stay in their villas and hotels, are enchanted by the Old Town, the countryside covered in olive trees, the monasteries and palaces, and the views and beaches. Even though it has cash problems it is a very safe destination. The island is like a ripe red apple, ready for eating. But inside the apple it is rotting. The coaches from the cruise ships pass along the coast and see the nightclub strip closed – it is daytime. Come by at night and the clubs are still closed: locals have no money to enjoy the music. Other roads out of town will tell the same story: there are many empty shops. But there is something more worrying, which is not seen by the visitors: the friendly Greeks are now less friendly to each other as trust is breaking down.

Let me return to 1962 and remember my lift on the autobahn just before arriving in Denmark. The driver of the Mercedes said: '*Adenauer lieber De Gaulle.*' The love between nations in Europe is now breaking down.

Fast forward to Sunday 12th July 2015. Jannie and I were driving to Denmark to see friends and family. I phoned our daughter Louise to say we were fine and she replied: 'Have you heard the news? Angela Merkel is kicking Greece out of Europe. Don't you spend anything in Germany,' she added.

My problem with Louise's suggestion was that we were staying over night in Lubeck.

We left the hotel to go to the Schiffergesellschaft Restaurant. I approached the first German we met as we crossed into the city to give him a piece of my mind, but he was drunk.

The Restaurant was originally the huge saloon where the sailors and fishermen of this lovely Hanseatic City would meet after arriving back in port.

'How are you, sir?' asked the manager.

I replied: 'Today the love of my life is dying'. He was shocked. He took us to one of the long tables beside which other diners were sitting on benches.

I repeated my answer to our waitress as she took our order. 'Europe is dying!' She was even more shocked. 'I hear that Angela Merkel is kicking Greece out of Europe', I added.

The man sitting next to us decided to join in. 'It is not Chancellor Merkel but Wolfgang Schäuble who wants them to leave. A lot of Germans agree. The news was in today's *Frankfurter Allgemeine Zeitung*.'

'And what do you know about Greece?' I replied. There was silence so I felt it was time to educate him. I told him:

'Three years ago Corfu had three levels of government; now it has only one.' As there was no reaction I continued:

'Two years ago my bank on the island wouldn't give me any of my money.' The German smiled. 'Because I had not given it my tax number. And does your government access people's bank accounts?' He did not answer so I added:

'Last year they wouldn't give me any money again.' He smiled again. 'Because I had not given them my UK pension details.'

I summed up my argument: 'Greece has started to sort itself out. So why keep punishing the Greeks?'

He replied: 'Because there are rules. We don't trust the Greeks.'

I was furious so I told him: 'If Britain heard that the Germans were now the bosses of Europe and kicking others out, then the British would react by leaving.'

LIFE IN A FINANCIAL GREEK TRAGEDY

The man was on the defensive and he added: 'I work for the government. Once the Greek situation has been sorted out, Chancellor Merkel and President Hollande will visit Prime Minister Cameron and we will work out how we can help him. We want Britain in Europe.'

So do I. But it must be a Europe that includes Greece and the poorer Mediterranean countries. I love Corfu with its incredible beauty. I love the Greeks with their dancing and the music in their soul. But today they are sad. Tragically, it was when trust broke down between the Indian communities, that the divisions appeared which led to partition and tragedy.

As we left, our young waitress sweetly told me to wait until the morning. Thank goodness for the young.

Schäuble is 73, two years younger than me. As West Germany's interior minister in 1990, he sold off all the 'assets' of East Germany after the Wall came down. Now he was trying to do the same with Greek assets, starting with fourteen airports in Greece, which are being bought by the Germans at a knockdown price.

* * * * *

Days later our son, Peter, who had been staying in the little house we had built in 1970, phoned and told us about the termites in the roof. We immediately rushed out to Corfu.

We first visited Amalia, our accountant, whose son is only a few years old. She was almost in tears as she told us about the situation:

'Times are bad in Greece now. People can only get €420 (£300) a week out of the bank. The capital controls are wrecking the country. Nobody is paying me, so how can I pay my staff.' I told her about our Lubeck experience. She replied: 'The foreign press are spreading lies about Greece'.

We knew this. We had warned Peter what the *Telegraph* had printed: 'The Foreign Office is preparing to issue new travel advice to British holidaymakers facing the prospect of a run on the banks and riots on the streets in Greece as the country heads for economic meltdown.

'With Greece on the brink of leaving the euro, the Foreign Office in London said its official advice for travellers was "under review"'.

'Although officials will wait to draft the advice until the situation in southern Europe becomes clearer, they are considering "all sorts of issues". This includes the potential for cash machines to shut if Greece reneges on its debts and violent protests should the Left-wing Syriza government bow to its creditors' demands, a spokesman said.'

We were worried about Elena, the widow of the Corfiot who had welcomed us to the island in 1966. Well into her eighties, she needed a Zimmer frame to move around. We took her to the magical Nautilus Restaurant at the end of the Garitsa Bay, which was full of gin-palaces and mega-yachts. I wondered how many of the owners had paid their taxes.

Her problem was simple to define but difficult to solve. 'The 420 euros from my pension and savings does not cover my rent, my carer, the food and other bills. Do I down-size to save money?'

She lived in a one-bedroom flat in the town centre. Moving at her age would have been a death warrant.

'Or do I get rid of the carer? Perhaps I could have her half-time but there would be no other work for her in Corfu so she would probably go back to Albania. John, I lived through the German occupation in the War and the poverty in Athens now compares with those times.' Twice a week we took Elena out to Nautilus and the conversation didn't change at first. Then she asked where she could change some pound notes into euros. 'If my carer took them into a bank they would ask her where she got them from.' Only after hearing this story a few times did we realise she was begging us to help. We exchanged £60 and she was really grateful. 'Now I can pay my telephone bill.'

Greek pensioners, whose retirement age of 67 is the oldest in Europe although some like those in the merchant marine retire early in a similar way that British firemen retire at 55, are receiving a continuously reducing pension. They can barely afford to live with VAT being raised on everything including food. Often they have to support their unemployed children and grandchildren. Total unemployment in Greece is officially at 29%, higher than in the great US Depression, and youth unemployment is over 50%. Realistically less than half the population is properly employed.

Nikos, our engineer, visited our house and concluded that we did not have termites but nests of insects under the roof tiles. They were probably ants and were not eating the roof. We sat and enjoyed Jannie's famous Chicken and Asparagus Salad and looked out to sea. He told us his best friend was emigrating to Sweden as doctors were no longer being paid. There were hundreds like him leaving the health service as there was no money.

He told us that thousands of small Greek companies had already left for Bulgaria because taxes were rocketing. 29% of their income had to be paid for this year, plus 29% for next year in advance. And every company, however small, had to pay a flat €650 tax as well. The typical self-employed Greek was packing up work.

Capital controls were making it difficult for firms to buy raw materials from abroad or sell finished products to overseas buyers. Imports and exports would fall and Greece would have even more difficulty paying its way.

Nikos and a team at the university had invented a prototype, which used the sun and chemicals to convert waste products into 'Sun Gas'. He was certain that this invention was the future of local, low-cost alternative energy production. But Brussels was no longer keeping to its agreement under the National Strategic Reference Framework (NSRF or ESPA in Greek) where the Government and European Regional

Development Fund split investment 50:50, to pay the university; so it could not make a production unit.

He said we should be doing what Germany does, not what German says: invest in the future, not cut, cut, cut. Across the length and breadth of Germany, there are thousands of wind turbines and millions of solar panels. One of Greece's major assets is the sun. My own hobbyhorse is with solar power. All those mentioned in the last chapter from Slovenia, Croatia and Montenegro wholeheartedly agree.

Why invest in solar projects in the Sahara, where sand storms can etch the solar panels and where terrorists can destroy the solar farms? Why not invest in Greece with panels installed beside the 400-mile long Egnatia Way, which can be connected to Austria by a submarine cable laid along the eastern Adriatic coast?

The cable would also receive out-of-season electricity from the less populated Balkan countries with their seasonal influx of tourists in the summer. It would consist of solar panels along its length, wind energy from the strong autumn, winter and spring Bura winds and hydro in the spring from the mountains in the hinterland. Out of the tourist season the electricity would be sent to the colder northern countries. The length of the cable in Greece is the same as that from the UK to Norway, which is planned for 2020. Already Norwegian and German operators have agreed to build a cable transmitting up to 1,400 MW between the two countries by 2018. Such investment will provide jobs for engineers, farmers and mechanics. It will provide warmth for the cold north in the winter. In January and February 2015, Slovenia lost 25% of its power as the country froze under a blanket of ice, which destroyed trees and brought down power lines. Perhaps Siemens could contribute to the cost from the profit it made from the Olympic Games?

* * * * *

LIFE IN A FINANCIAL GREEK TRAGEDY

Europe will succeed if we work together and if no single country tries to run the show. Look back to 1962 and our trip through Yugoslavia, where one part, Serbia, tried to rule the roost.

The Germans may not trust the Greeks, but now the Greeks do not trust the Germans either.

The *Guardian* put it perfectly: 'The ruthlessness that her finance minister, Wolfgang Schäuble, displayed in bouncing Greece into total capitulation at the July summit, has done lasting damage to Germany's reputation for giving Europe a lead that can transcend petty national rivalries'.

Comments by individual Greeks when I mentioned Schäuble reminded me of 1966, soon after German occupation in World War Two and the civil war that followed, and should be a warning to Germany and for the future of Europe.

An elderly architect said: '*Deutschland Über Alles*'.

A young waiter said: 'From our Independence when we had a German king, we have always had foreigners running our country.' Referring to a computer game he added: 'We are the Mouse in the Labyrinth.'

A middle-aged clerk pulled a Stanley knife out from under her counter at the mention of Schäuble's name.

Just before the end of our visit to our second home, Jannie and I went to all the booksellers on the island to collect our money. All their records were perfectly in order. They all paid me. Conversation turned to the crisis. One of them who is a highly intelligent man, speaks excellent English and is proud of his country, shocked me by what he said. Afterwards I showed his words to a dozen Corfiots, some professionals and others not, and they all agreed with the sentiments.

I had asked his young son which he preferred: Panathanaikos or Olympiakos, the top two Greek football teams. The boy replied that he preferred school and showed me his homework.

His father then said: 'It is better that way. I think about

his future, it is not good in Greece. Of course over the years we have made mistakes, many have dodged paying taxes, and the politicians and others have been corrupt. Now we must be given a chance. We cannot survive more and more taxes and more and more cuts.'

He paused.

'Perhaps there is just one cut I would accept. Someone to cut Schäuble's throat!'

* * * * *

Friday 30th October was a busy day at the bank. On the last day of the month, Greeks pay their taxes. Every bank in Corfu was full, some with queues starting outside. We waited in line for just under two hours to hand over cash for the house tax. The record we were told was a seven-hour wait. The bank manager's job was crowd control; he decided who was guilty when a fight started over who was jumping the queue. The pensioners were there to collect their weekly money.

Exhausted we made for the best food on the island in a restaurant 25 metres from the market. Some ten years ago 40-year-old Stamatis Vasilakis, took over from his father who, in 1965 after managing the restaurant, bought *Rouvas* from the owner who founded the original taverna in 1936. He kept the name and the next generation now cook the same fantastically flavoursome foods as in years gone past. Many of the vegetables are grown on the family farm in Zigos, high on the Pantokrator Massif. One of the strengths of Greece is the family.

Jannie chose chicken in a lemon sauce and I had *stifado*, slow-cooked braised beef with shallots and garlic in a piquant sauce. Let Stamatis have the last word about my beloved Greece:

'The last two years have been very hard for Greece. The system is broken. It must change or we should start again.'

AN OPEN LETTER TO CHANCELLOR MERKEL

In September 1962 I was in Bavaria returning from hitch hiking (*autostop*) to India. The driver of my lift said: '*Adenaur lieber De Gaulle*'. As a 22 year-old, his statement was the foundation of my life-long love of Germany and Europe.

On Sunday July 12th 2015 my wife and I were staying in Lübeck and heard that Wolfgang Schäuble wanted to kick Greece out of the Eurozone if the Greek government would not undertake more drastic reforms. Just days after the Greek people had rejected Europe's austerity terms Alexis Tsipras performed a u-turn and produced a new set of tough reform proposals very similar to those he had just campaigned against. On Friday July 10th, the Greek parliament gave Tsipras an overwhelming majority in support of his proposals.

Whilst we were having a meal at the *Schiffergesellschaft* Restaurant, you and Tsipras were negotiating for more than 10 hours. Tsipras could not accede to Schäuble's Luxembourg trust fund, which he saw as an outrageous European attempt to pilfer the Greek family silver. Nobody could imagine where Greece was going to find €50bn in assets to privatise, and the idea of surrendering them to a trust fund in Luxembourg was an insult to which no government could possibly agree. In the end, Tsipras capitulated to a script written in Berlin.

In June you personally invited 800,000 refugees to Germany in a repeat of the 1960s *Gastarbeiter* programme. You said: '*Wir schaffen das*'. We have just returned from Greece via Montenegro, Croatia, Slovenia and Germany.

Greece is in the front-line, accepting these refugees. I do not think Greece can cope with the financial and refugee crisis. I ask you to help them, particularly over writing off their mountain of debt.

One day I hope to hear '*Angela Merkel lieber Alexis Tsipras*'.

November 2015,

John Waller, yiannisbooks@aol.com

BOOKS BY JOHN WALLER

Greek Walls – an Odyssey in Corfu 2004
'Often funny, always informative' The Corfiot
'Most enjoyable read' Lesley Toll, Daily Mail

Corfu Sunset – Avrio never comes 2005
'A highly amusing account of the highs and lows of property ownership abroad' Evening Standard
'Reveals with panache and passion the rewards and drawbacks of buying property in a remote place' Nigel Lewis, Daily Mail

Irish Flames – the Arrival of the Black and Tans 2006
'Anybody with even a little Irish blood in his or her veins will find this story a remarkable account of the end of British Rule' The Irish Post

Corfu Sketches – A Thirty-year Journey with sketches 2008, by Theresa Nicholas and text by John Waller
'A remarkable book' Anglo-Hellenic Review

Corfu Town Walks – 8 pages laminated A5 walks 2009

Walking the Corfu Trail – with Friends, Flowers and Food 2010
'No one feels the beat of Corfu's heart more keenly than John Waller' Mark Palmer, Daily Mail

Atlantic Affair 2013
'I thoroughly enjoyed reading Atlantic Affair, the story of one of Ireland's three greatest yachtsmen' Marcus Connaughton, RTE Seascapes
'An invention which is of vital interest to sea-going yachtsmen' The Tatler 1931

Details of the above are on www.yiannisbooks.com

John Waller was born in Hythe, Kent in 1940 to an Irish sportsman and builder. He was evacuated to Cornwall. After Cambridge University, he trained as an engineer at IBM and set up and ran a successful computer company in 1969. In 1970, he and his Danish wife built a minute house in Corfu, where he has written his seven non-fiction books after his retirement in 1999. He was Liberal Democrat Parliamentary Candidate for Twickenham in 1979, 1983 and 1987.